Save the World

Working to help others

By Jane Lyons

Australia

Published by Career FAQs Pty Ltd

Published by
Career FAQs Pty Ltd
Suite 76, The Hub
89–97 Jones Street
Ultimo NSW 2007
+61 2 9282 9383
www.careerfaqs.com.au

National Library of Australia
Cataloguing-in-Publication entry:

Lyons, Jane

Save the World: working to help others.

ISBN 978 1 921106 262

1. Nonprofit organisations – Vocational guidance –
Australia. 2. Charities – Vocational guidance – Australia.
I. Title.

331.1241361763

Publisher: Sue Stevens
Author: Jane Lyons
Editor: Emma Grahame
Editorial assistants: Darryn King and Alison Edwards
Production coordinator: Louisa Veidelis
Production assistants: Jacob Sheen and Bill Birtles
Cover and internal design: Terri Marzullo, H2M Creative Services
Illustrations: Tamsin Ainslie, Ainslie Beard Creative
Desktop publisher: Terri Marzullo, H2M Creative Services
Printed by Paragon Printers Australasia
Advertising sales: Stef Harland

Career FAQs acknowledges the following copyright owners for permission to reproduce their work.

Challenge Consulting Australia

National Roundtable of Non-profit Organisations

Elizabeth Cham, NRNO

Ted Flack, Queensland University of Technology

Every effort has been made to contact copyright owners and obtain permission. However, should an infringement have occurred, Career FAQs apologises for the omission and requests that the copyright owner contact them.

Disclaimer

The opinions and statements made by people who contributed to this book are their own and are not those of Career FAQs. The publishers do not claim to represent the entire extent of the not-for-profit/aid industries and career choices. The aim has always been to provide a broad overview of the possibilities available.

As such Career FAQs *Save the World* does not purport to be a true and accurate record of the not-for-profit/aid industry, relying on the voices of those working in the industry to tell their stories. Inaccuracies may arise as a result of the nature of this book. Users should follow the links to actual websites of organisations to ascertain current information.

 An imprint of Career FAQs

Foreword

When it comes to 'saving the world', there is much work to be done.

Despite our best efforts, poverty, hunger, disease, illiteracy, environmental degradation and discrimination against women remain the hallmarks of many parts of the world. At home, the search for cures to a myriad of diseases is ongoing, elderly people require care, homeless people require support and many other people in our community need a hand.

The not-for-profit sector plays a big part in this ongoing battle, and its growth in the last decade has seen career visions change and options broaden.

More and more professionals are choosing to work in this area. For many, a career in the not-for-profit sector is a rare privilege, and an opportunity to align their personal values with the values of their employer and to provide a service that really makes a difference.

This sector is made up of organisations from the humanitarian arena, community-based organisations, educational institutions, the health care sector and many more. All too often they have limited resources, staff and budgets, so the demand for high-quality staff driven by values and commitment is often greater than the commercial sector.

There is no standard training or qualification to work in these organisations. Lawyers, engineers, marketers, teachers, doctors, nurses, journalists, accountants and many more are all needed.

However, the traits that people working in the not-for-profit sector do have in common are extraordinary professionalism, flexibility, resilience and good humour. They share the aim of enjoying a satisfying career that involves lifestyle choices and a commitment to making a positive difference in the world.

If you are looking for a job 'saving the world', I'd encourage you to study in a field that you enjoy and are good at, with the objective of becoming highly skilled in that chosen area. At the same time, get as much voluntary experience as you can with not-for-profit agencies so you know which part of the sector you would suited best. This is your first step towards a diverse, challenging and fulfilling career that will impact humanity.

Carolyn Hardy, CEO,

UNICEF Australia

Carolyn Hardy is Chief Executive of UNICEF Australia, her role being to fundraise and advocate for UNICEF projects aimed at ensuring the rights and survival of vulnerable children all over the world.

Prior her to appointment at UNICEF, she held senior marketing positions with The Australian Financial Review newspaper. She has a Bachelor of Arts degree majoring in Journalism, a Master of Arts degree and a Post Graduate Diploma of Management.

Carolyn is currently a member of the Executive Committee of the Australia Council for International Development and she is a member of the National Advisory Group for Australia's report on the Convention of the Rights of the Child.

Contents

Insider info

Ready, set, go for it!

About Career FAQs

Whether you are just starting out, changing jobs, moving up the ladder or returning to work after a break, Career FAQs books give the inside story on just about any job you can imagine.

> Don't end up in someone else's life.
> A career choice is really a life choice.
> Will Santow, Managing Director, Career FAQs

What makes our books different?

❝Career FAQs is Australia's leading careers publisher, with a dynamic new approach to making career choices.❞

In each book, employees, employers, recruiters and industry experts tell their stories – so you can really tell if this is the right career for you. You'll find out what is happening right now in your chosen area, get the inside info on the qualifications you need and where to get them, and find out what current employees really love about their jobs.

You also find out how to stand out from the crowd and get that dream job, with our industry-specific résumé, cover letter and interview tips and examples.

Career FAQs is Australia's leading careers publisher, with a dynamic new approach to making career choices.

> I started Career FAQs because of my own difficulties in finding empowering, high-quality, up-to-date career information to help me make career decisions.

> I wanted to change careers in my 30s, but trying to research a new direction led to a dead end – there was no interesting and reliable information on the qualifications I needed for different jobs, the opportunities available, likelihood of succeeding, or, most importantly, what the work would be like once I got there.

> I know that our books can make such choices easier by giving our readers the information they need to find a career that meets their dreams and aspirations.

Our range covers the usual career areas, as well as moving well beyond ordinary categories into careers you may never have thought of. There's a great job out there waiting for you and we can show you what it is and how to get it.

A big thanks goes out to the many people who have taken the time to talk to us and shared their experiences with our readers, as well as to the many eminent Australians who have written forewords to our books, sharing the insight and wisdom that has helped take them to the top.

For a list of current titles, please visit our website, www.careerfaqs.com.au.

With Career FAQs you have all the tools to find your dream job.

Good luck!

Will Santow
Managing Director
Career FAQs

How to use this book

All Career FAQs books are carefully structured to help you find the information you need quickly and easily.

You'll find three main sections.

'The big picture' provides an overview of the industry, including employment opportunities and income snapshots. You'll find information about the main employers and support organisations, as well as interviews with employers about what they look for.

'Insider info' contains interviews that recount the personal experiences of people who are currently working in the job, profession or industry. It allows you to discover what it is really like to work at various levels of seniority.

'Ready, set, go for it!' tells you how to get the appropriate training and experience for the job and what to do to get your dream job. You'll find out how to create your application and how to stand out at interviews.

These are the icons we use in our books to help you navigate. Some may not appear in every book.

 is a snapshot of each interviewee's career pathway – it shows some of the stepping stones along the career path that led to their current position

 directs you to another Career FAQs title that might interest you

 tells you where to find out more about a particular topic or organisation

 provides interesting additional information, which might come in handy!

 provides a brief definition of a word, term or acronym that appears in bold in the text

Many words, phrases, abbreviations and acronyms are defined in buzz words at the back of this book.

brief sums up a specific job, including salary, qualifications, number of hours worked, life–work balance and flexibility, as told by our interviewee

 explodes a popular myth about the industry or profession

myweek gives you a day-by-day overview of the typical tasks involved in this job and how they interact with life in general

myday gives you an outline of a day in the job

The big picture

Why save the world?

Are you more into making a difference than making a quick buck? Passionate about the environment, helping sick kids or building houses for refugees? Perhaps you're put off by the idea of the nine-to-five grind – whatever your motivation, it's time to get serious about the world around you.

Ignore those who tell you to get a haircut and get a real job. For more and more people, saving the world is a real job.

There are loads of not-for-profit organisations – or **NFP**s – that offer people the opportunity to combine passion, principle and career. Whatever your passion may be, there is sure to be an organisation for you: from the environment, social justice and animal rights to health, youth and Indigenous affairs.

Saving the world isn't just about rattling a donation tin at passers-by on the street. While advocacy work, campaigning and fundraising are integral to what these organisations do, there's also demand for people with management, accounting, administration, IT, nursing, marketing and journalism skills, to name just a few.

glossary

NFP means:
– not-for-profit organisation.

Although you're not likely to wipe out world debt with your first years' wages, the pay in the not-for-profit sector is not bad either – and, more importantly, the biggest reward is a powerful sense of achievement that comes from knowing your work is helping others.

SAVE THE WORLD

This book focuses on individuals working for NFP and government-funded volunteer organisations both in Australia and overseas. You'll see what it's like to give your time, knowledge and energy to something bigger than yourself – something that could really have an impact.

In saying that, you don't have to be Mother Teresa to have a go at saving the world – as all of the people interviewed confirm, every small step counts. Mahatama Gandhi said, 'Be the change you want to see in the world' – and there's no time like the present to start!

It's not what you do, but why you do it

Of course, everybody has their own idea of how to make a difference – be it joining a local tree planting group, running a charitable website or working as a nurse in Africa.

What is central to this career path is not so much what people do as their motivation for doing it. Having three televisions and a jacuzzi is

not the highest priority here. Altruism – the belief in unselfish action for the benefit of others – is one of the dominant factors in choosing an NFP career.

> There's a groundswell of people recognising that there's more to life than just working and earning money. Young people are exposed to the consumer revolution in their teens and have seen that it's really not that satisfying. There's now more recognition of the value of giving and helping others.
> Elizabeth Cham, Philanthropy Australia

Helping others not only feels good; it can be good for you, too. Stephen Post from Case Western Reserve University in the US specialises in collating research on altruism and its relation to mental and physical health. He has noted a strong correlation between the happiness, health and longevity of people who are emotionally and behaviourally compassionate, provided they aren't overwhelmed by it.

MYTH

NFPs are disorganised

fact

While they can be less-structured and more flexible, NFPs still need to be efficient and effective.

NFP organisations

NFP organisations (NFPs) belong to the sector also known as the 'third sector'. According to Mark Lyons, an expert on the area, we normally divide the world of organisations into two sectors – government and business – ignoring this third and very distinct sector.

> NFP organisations are the product of people's commitment to providing a service for others, to represent their interests or lobby on behalf of others, or to practise a religion. They are not part of government, even though they may perform a public service; neither are they established or operated to make a profit for their owners.
> Mark Lyons, Author, *Third Sector*

All proceeds are funnelled back into the organisation so they can be used for the services that it provides. Although some staff members are paid a salary, there are no shareholders or profit-sharing schemes. Money is not the reward.

These organisations are many and varied and can include anything from schools and credit unions to trade unions and professional associations. However, the organisations we will be focusing on include those involved in community services, health and public interest. These types of organisations are often referred to as NGOs or non-government organisations.

What do people in the NFP sector do?

This is like asking, 'How long is a piece of string?' or, 'How wide is the universe?' If your imagination can stretch to it, someone's probably out there doing it. There's a niche to suit every personality – whether you're a bit off the wall or prefer to toe the straight and narrow.

To find out about the different things that people do, we asked the people interviewed for this book. Here's some of the things they said.

- Monitor, analyse and comment on the impact of government's responses to human rights and humanitarian law
- Undertake security training, risk management protocols and crisis response management
- Manage staff, liaise with campaigners, take care of the daily needs of clients
- Hire and fire employees, deal with regulators, maintain training standards
- Design, monitor, implement and evaluate projects
- Educate patients and parents, counselling patients and families
- Raise funds, write sponsorship proposals
- Write articles for in-house publications, design newsletters, source merchandise
- Design and maintain websites, edit content
- Undertake PR exercises and other media-related work

While the motives that drive NFPs are altruistic, they all have to run efficiently to stay in business. As this list shows, this means they need to have all the components of a business operation.

detour

There is a career book about working in design, education, public relations and just about any other career you can think of. Check them out on our website.

www.careerfaqs.com.au

What personal qualities best suit this sector?

We asked people working in various jobs in the NFP sector what personal characteristics and attributes are suited to charitable work. Below are just some of the qualities they highlighted.

- Ability to focus on the task at hand
- Perseverance and professionalism
- Adaptability and a positive attitude
- Stamina – mental, emotional and physical
- Commitment to the cause
- Being a 'people' person
- Genuine empathy and patience
- Passion for all things philanthropic
- Love of the work, not money
- Thrift and creativity
- Lack of greed and no interest in power
- Progressive politics
- Approachability and confidence
- Clear vision and sense of perspective

Clearly, there is a strong emphasis on interpersonal skills and personal motivation – the thing about working in this sector is that your work, when it comes down to it, isn't all about you.

Compassion fatigue

While commitment to a cause can be fulfilling, compassion fatigue is something that can knock you about no matter how lofty your principles. Dealing with sick children, desperately poor people or wounded animals on a daily basis can all cause burnout – and it's nothing to be ashamed of. Many NFPs struggle with this issue, and scarce resources, staff cutbacks and poor funding don't help.

> As we struggle with these outside realities, the needs of those we serve continue to become more urgent and complex. It seems there is always hurting, always need, and often more bad news than good. Feelings of defeat and desperation can cause tremendous stress for managers, employees and volunteers of charities and NFP organisations. This stress, if unchecked, can become chronic, leading to apathy, depression and ultimately, burnout.
>
> Kristin Duare McKinnon, *Coping with Caring – the dangers of chronic stress and burnout*, Pathways

Life–work balance, therefore, is especially important in the NFP sector. It's vital to be able to look out for yourself before you can help others. An unhealthy and unhappy worker is not going to be much help to anyone.

What's happening right now?

The late 60s and early 70s saw a sea change in official attitudes to social welfare. Governments around the world decided – for better or worse – that instead of bogging themselves down with huge welfare services and associated bureaucracies, they would divert a portion of taxpayers' money to independent charities. Ted Flack describes the trend as an attempt by governments to 'steer things rather than row'.

This means that, instead of running employment and housing agencies and services for disadvantaged youth, Indigenous health and the like, the government concentrates on providing the funding – while the NFPs actually run the services. Under these circumstances philanthropic groups flourish and expand into the far-reaching networks that they are today, and they continue to grow.

fyi

The Australian Youth Ambassadors for Development program is an example of a government –NGO partnership. Meet one of its workers in 'Insider info'.

'As government does less and less, NFPs are springing up to fill the gaps,' says Brett de Hoedt of Hootville Communications, a public relations company that specialises in the NFP sector.

Increased wealth in Australia and the developed world in the past 40 years has also been a factor in fostering the growth of charitable organisations. As they become more affluent, communities are starting to think about how they can help improve the quality of life of others in less fortunate circumstances – be it health, environment, poverty, community development or social justice.

> The sector has definitely grown ... environment groups are abounding with the tangible impact of green house gases and water issues; self-help groups continue to expand as people seek out mutual support.
> Rhonda Galbally, CEO, Our Community

SAVE THE WORLD WITH CARE

Professionalism

The terms 'entrepreneur' and 'not for profit' may seem at odds with each other given that entrepreneurs are often associated with ability to make big money quickly. However, given that most charities rely either solely or partly on fundraising, the ability to make money is a major priority. The difference is that the money is going to a good cause.

Ted Flack from the Centre of Philanthropy and Not-for-Profit Studies in Queensland sees entrepreneurs as people who create new environments, not just churn out money.

MYTH

charity work is all about door-knocking

There are heaps of career opportunities for high flyers in this sector – it's an exciting, dynamic area in which to build a fulfilling career.

fact

> Entrepreneurs – those who want to put things together to make a new world – are not motivated just by money but by the way in which they interact with world in a social and political sense.
>
> Ted Flack, Centre of Philanthropy and NFP Studies , QUT

In this sense, NFP organisations are populated by business people serving the greater good rather than some money-hungry industry. They need to be tuned in to the world of commerce as well as community in order for their organisations to operate effectively. This is where the concept of professionalism comes in.

> The notion that charities are run and operated on a shoestring by high-minded individuals who all just want to do a wonderful job for the community is still there, but it's no longer the dominant paradigm. The dominant paradigm these days is the professionalisation of charities.
>
> Ted Flack, Centre of Philanthropy and NFP Studies, QUT

And while volunteers still make up a large part of the NFP sector, especially the smaller organisations, demand for staff with professional expertise is on the rise. It's a question of survival.

> Those NFP organisations that operate on blood, sweat and tears won't last very long. The number of people who need their services is not declining, so they've got to find ways to do more with less. They have to have sophisticated systems of managing the organisation that are competitive with other sectors.
>
> Denis Flores, Organisational psychologist

As the Bob Dylan song goes, the times, they are a-changin' – and no-one knows that better than the fundraising manager for the Salvation Army, Sam Broughton. Initially a volunteer with the Red Cross, Sam has spent all his working life in NFPs.

With no formal training in fundraising or public relations, he has had to rely on his sense of empathy and social justice. These days, as Sam himself admits, it's more important to recruit people with tertiary qualifications and therefore increase the organisation's potential business success even more.

> If charities want to compete and operate successfully, they have to move away from people of just good will to people with more formal qualifications.
>
> Sam Broughton, Fundraising manager, Salvation Army

At the other end of the spectrum, Rhonda Galbally – who runs the support organisation **Our Community** – warns that, in small NFPs in particular, it's not always a question of formal qualifications.

> On the one hand, there are the community service agencies where staff must be professionally trained in things such as social work and alcohol and drug rehabilitation. On the other hand, there are small community groups that place less emphasis on professional qualifications – particularly when it comes to part-time roles – but the skills employees demonstrate are nonetheless significant (such as financial and risk management, communication and marketing).
>
> Rhonda Galbally, Our Community

These days, it seems that working for NFPs requires a combination of passion and practical skills, with one augmenting the other.

Partnering up

As well as cooperation with governments, NFPs have increasingly sought private enterprise partnerships with firms from the corporate sector, with the aim of improving services, expanding networks and broadening their skills base.

And with the rapidly growing influence of **CSR** – the business buzzword of the moment – many companies have jumped on board. Some now allow their employees to spend up to two years working for a NFP.

glossary

CSR means:

– corporate social responsibility, that is, the commitment of businesses to contribute to sustainable economic development, local communities and society at large to improve their quality of life.

SAVE THE WORLD WITH PASSION

Current size of the sector

There are about 35 000 NFP organisations in Australia that employ full-time paid staff.

The total number of NFP organisations in Australia is around 700 000. Many of these are small and entirely dependent on the voluntary commitment of members. This number includes any and every organisation that operates on a not-for-profit basis, including weekend sporting clubs and special interest groups.

According to the National Roundtable of Non-profit Organisations (NRNO) in 1999–2000, NFPs:

- employ 604 000 people, 6.8 per cent of Australians in employment

- have a combined yearly income of $33.5 billion

- contributed $21 billion (3.3 per cent) to GDP

- make an economic contribution larger than the communications industry and about equal to that of the agriculture industry – a contribution almost twice as large as the entire economic contribution of Tasmania.

A fact sheet released by the NRNO divides the sector into six areas of service providers. The following chart shows the percentage of workers in each area.

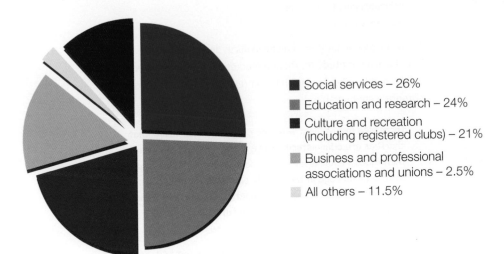

- Social services – 26%
- Education and research – 24%
- Culture and recreation (including registered clubs) – 21%
- Business and professional associations and unions – 2.5%
- All others – 11.5%

Types of organisations in the sector
Source: National Roundtable of Non-profit Organisations, www.nfproundtable.org.au

Like many businesses in the corporate world, the NFP sector is currently faced with labour shortages. This may be partly due to the retirement of the baby boomers, but can also be attributed to the rapid professionalisation of the sector.

> There is an emphasis on qualifications and skills. It used to be that just offering help was enough, but now there's the realisation that we need people who actually have qualifications or relevant work experience.
>
> Trish McDonald, HR officer, CARE Australia

The provision of health services is in particular a rapidly expanding area. The onset of the **wellness revolution** combined with recently increased awareness of health problems like obesity and heart disease in Australia mean that there is massive opportunity for qualified candidates looking to get a foot in the door.

Environmental promotion and conservation, international aid and community services are also growth industries.

fyi

Baby boomers are those post-World War II babies born between 1946 and 1960 – making the youngest boomers 46 in 2006.

glossary

Wellness revolution means:

– the current trend of good living and healthy eating. It is expected to generate a net worth of a trillion dollars in the US over the next decade, and $75 billion in Australia.

> Overall, community service non-profits are growing, although parts of childcare are shrinking. The general charity organisation is growing. So too are health charities and self-help organisations like the Cancer Council, Heart Foundation and schizophrenia fellowships.
>
> Mark Lyons, Author, *Third Sector*

There are also a number of niche skills in demand. If you're qualified in or have an aptitude for PR and marketing, for example, your skills will be highly valued by an NFP that relies on public donations and corporate sponsorship.

detour

Interested in finding aout about jobs in the sectors? Check out Career FAQs *Marketing* and *Public Relations*

www.careerfaqs.com.au

> Increased involvement with the community has meant that charities are administering more modern PR and marketing techniques. People are more responsive to this kind of approach, so to keep an edge in the heavily competitive NFP space, organisations will be seeking competent PR and marketing professionals more and more in the future.
>
> John Dalziel, former media manager, Salvation Army

Specialised fundraising skills are also highly in demand, according to Sam Broughton, the Salvation Army's fundraising manager. Meanwhile, social work skills have been in such short supply that Barnardos has set up its own recruitment service, SocialWorks, which specialises in the area.

> There is a chronic employment shortage in the sector, so we are trying to raise the profile of social work by showing up at university career fairs and also trying to attract trained people from overseas.
>
> Carol Lockley, Manager, SocialWorks

> Campaigners are probably most in demand. Generally the money that is offered is less than what can be earned in other sectors, so there is a tendency for less experienced persons to apply. In reality campaigning organisations need a strong proportion of experienced staff as well as the capacity for building recruits.
>
> Lyn Goldsworthy, NFP consultant

John Peacock from NFP Analysts says the sector is moving increasingly online, making web design and IT skills highly sought after. People with good business skills are also more important than ever.

Andi Pannell spent three years managing up to 80 volunteers for the Starlight Children's Foundation. She was awarded a scholarship by the Australian Graduate School of Management for students in the NFP sector and is now doing a Master of Businees Administration (MBA).

I really feel that the NFP sector lacks people with solid business experience, and as these organisations grow there aren't enough people there with business skills who can effectively manage that growth.

If I can get some really solid corporate experience and then go back to an NFP I think I'd be a really valuable asset.

Andi Pannell, MBA student

Some of the 'in demand' jobs in the NFP sector are shown in the following table.

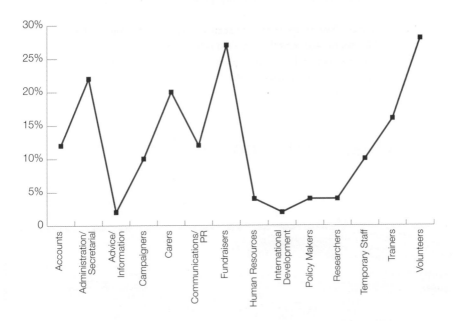

Areas of difficulty in recruiting

Source: Challenge Consulting Australia, NFP Industry Survey Report, January 2006

You can see from this survey that fundraising is the most troublesome recruitment area, with administration and carer jobs next in line. Volunteering is another area in which it's difficult to fill positions. Traditionally, this has been the domain of married women who do not work. With more women entering the paid workforce in the last half of the last century, the recruitment of volunteers has been badly in need of a makeover. Many organisations such as Médecins Sans Frontières look to recruit volunteers for short periods in a mutually beneficial way – it helps the organisation gets things done while giving young people some valuable short-term experience.

Like the for-profit sector, the great majority of organisations employ less than 20 people. In almost all industries they are characterised by stressful and difficult work. If you are a manager, you are trying to juggle a lot of demands with limited income and if you are a frontline worker you are having a lot of pressure put on you to do more and more.

Mark Lyons, Author, *Third Sector*

Once an area that many moved into midway through their careers, the NFP sector now offers real choices for your first or second job – and there's no reason why you can't stay there!

Ten or 15 years ago it was not seen as long-term. Working in the NFP sector was something you did halfway through your working life; you came in from the corporate sector when you semi-retired. Now it's a career path.

Sam Broughton, Fundraising manager, Salvation Army

What are the job opportunities?

Here are just some oif the many interesting jobs that people are doing.

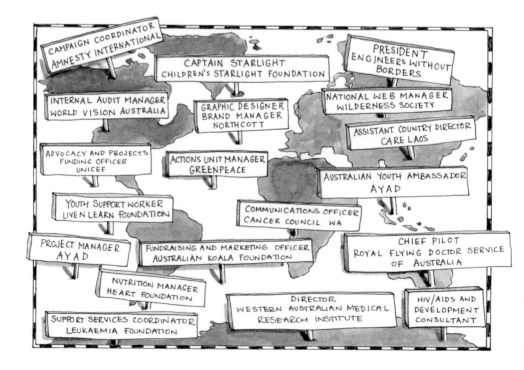

While you could probably hunt down a job that suits you in any sector, working for an NFP has that extra kick to it – the knowledge that every small success you have will result in positive change.

Whether working for a community-based organisation, an environmental group or health care charity, the opportunities are limitless. On the whole they fall into four basic categories:

- service delivery
- program design and policy advice
- corporate and administration support
- technical support.

Service delivery

These jobs focus on the core business of the organisation, such as: nurses, carers, field workers, social workers, counsellors, builders, engineers and vets. This work involves lots of interaction with individual clients or patients as well as with community groups and the general public.

While you could probably hunt down a job that suits you in any sector, working for an NFP has that extra kick to it – the knowledge that every small success you have will result in positive change.

Program design and policy advice

The people who work in this area decide what is needed and devise appropriate programs to address the problem. Essentially they are there to establish what the service deliverers will be doing and how they'll be doing it. This may involve training, developing and managing staff, analysing past successes or precedents, and trialling new solutions.

People working on policies may also work at a more overarching, strategic level in dealing with governments and other organisations to set goals, direction and vision.

Corporate and administration support

Every organisation needs the support of a management team and associated office administrators who look after the day-to-day running of the place. The general manager or chief executive officer usually heads a team that may include an accountant, a lawyer, administration assistants, IT people and many more.

This team is also likely to include the fundraisers who make sure there is ongoing financial support for the work and media and public relations people who ensure that the wider community knows about the organisation and supports its work.

Technical support

The rise and rise of technology is something it's been impossible to escape. Every business in the world now relies on it to operate more efficiently and effectively. Many businesses, even small ones, have their own website, and most staff use the Internet in some way or other on a regular basis.

As organisations become more reliant on technology, IT professionals are finding their skills and knowledge in high demand – and are well paid for their efforts.

Volunteers

The private and public sectors and NFPs differ in one very significant way – in the NFP sector it's both encouraged and expected that you'll have done some volunteer work to develop your skills and demonstrate your commitment.

Many people who have paid positions in an NFP started working as a volunteer. This way is to the paid workforce not only provides valuable experience but also shows a real willingness to work towards the organisation's purpose.

> You might have a volunteer board; you might have a membership base. To work successfully in the NFP sector you have to be able to work successfully with your paid employees, but also with the volunteer boards and management. Sometimes these volunteer boards and management don't have the skill base or competencies that you might have. So it's a real balancing act. You've really got to learn to deal with a huge range of stakeholders.
> Sam Broughton, Fundraising manager, Salvation Army

Whether the emphasis is on saving the environment, looking after the homeless, supporting those with cancer or servicing a myriad of other needs, NFP organisations focus more on people than money making, and this can have a flow-on effect for staff.

> There is more emphasis on regard for individuals and individual wellbeing, and that relates to the staff as well as the relationship to the clients.
>
> Denis Flores, Organisational psychologist

A sense of common purpose is also a unifying and powerful team-building force. When you meet the people in our 'Insider info' section, you'll notice that many speak of a sense of camaraderie that stems from working towards a shared goal.

> NFP organisations are a product of, and further encourage, people's capacity to work together to provide services for themselves or others, or to represent their interests to others, including government.
>
> Mark Lyons, Author, *Third Sector*

> The smaller working environment is an attractive quality of most NFPs – the individual is able to see the fruits of their labour more so than in a larger, publicly-listed organisation where they are less likely to make a visible impact. More often than not, the smaller environment also fosters a closer team approach.
>
> Peter Waite, Director, Waite Intersearch

Volunteers help out at a soup kitchen.

Gender balance

On the whole there are more women than men working in this sector, but men tend to occupy the more prominent CEO and senior management roles. Having said that, none of our interviewees reported discrimination or harassment and the number of women entering NFPs looks set to rise.

Some misconceptions still exist about the sector and the role of women in it. Many people are unaware of the rapid professionalisation of NFPs and dismiss them as lightweight women's volunteer 'hobbies', even though the sector is actually choc-a-block with highly qualified, skilled and committed women, many of them in leading roles.

> If I were a man, I do not believe I would be asked, 'Is that a full time job?' If you think of Tim Costello and World Vision, no-one would think he should be a volunteer – Red Cross too – but for smaller NFP companies I think there is an element that you should a) be paid less than in the 'real workforce' and b) that you should 'love your job more because you are making a difference'.
>
> Deborah Tabart, Chief executive officer, Australian Koala Foundation

Like in any job, if you have a family and children you may face difficulties juggling your work and home lives. Studies have shown that women in the NFP sector are more likely to be burdened with a heavy workload which can interfere with family life – particularly due to the amount of travel some positions may require. In addition to this it has been reported that the pay gap between men and women can be higher in the NFP sector than in the corporate world.

How much can I earn?

With the professionalisation of the sector has come the introduction of awards and enterprise agreements. Naturally, salaries vary according to the size of the organisation.

> The smaller groups with small budgets pay very low salaries and often the workers are part time – the conditions are not good and the work can be very stressful. At the other end of the spectrum, the large charities are paying premium salaries – competitive with medium-size business (with notable exceptions such as the Salvation Army, which has a moral position on the size of salaries).
>
> Rhonda Galbally, CEO, Our Community

The following table shows the salaries (or income bands) of the people interviewed for this book.

Age	Position title	Income A$	Time in job	Time in industry
20	Youth support worker	33 000 – 35 000	4 months	2 yrs
20–25	Communications officer	–	5 months	5 months
25	Captain Starlight	40 000	4 yrs	4 yrs
26	Advocacy and projects funding officer	45 000	5 months	3 yrs
26	Australian youth ambassador	Living allowance	<1	<1
26–30	Assistant country director	60 000 – 80 000	3 months	4 yrs
27	Fundraising & marketing officer	45 000 – 70 000	1 yr	–
Late 20s	Graphic designer, brand manager	34 000 – 45 000	2 yrs	2 yrs
29	Engineer	35 000	3 yrs	3 yrs
29	Project manager	60 000 – 90 000	8 months	5 yrs
32	Nutrition manager	–	3 yrs	–
36	Actions unit manager	63 000	2.5 yrs	13 yrs
36	Campaign coordinator	45 000 – 70 000	2 yrs	6 yrs
36	Internal audit manager	60 000 – 80 000	7 yrs	13 yrs
37	Support services coordinator	50 000	4 yrs	10 yrs
Early 40s	National web manager	40 000 – 50 000	–	–
48	Chief pilot	60 000 – 70 000	5.5 yrs	10 yrs
53	Director, medical research institute	150 000+	25 yrs	5 yrs

Career FAQs income snapshot, 2005–06

You can see that the incomes vary considerably depending on the type of work and the time in the job or in the industry. Of note is that the sector does enjoy benefits that public or private companies don't. Depending on their status with the Australian Tax Office, some organisations are classified as public benevolent institutions (PBIs), some are endorsed as rebatable employers for Fringe Benefits Tax (FBT) and others do not enjoy either status.

PBIs pay no FBT and can offer employees untaxed benefits of up to $30 000 per annum. Some employers may be eligible as rebate FBT employers and pay only half the FBT they would normally – so the employee pays no personal tax on the fringe benefit of up to $15 000 per annum.

Both these options can be delivered in a variety of forms. Generally, rebatable employers will establish an account for each employee, into which the fringe benefit is deposited. Sometimes a credit card is linked to this account and given to the employee to spend as they wish. (The interest charges are deducted from the fringes benefits.) Some employees arrange for their employer to pay personal bills out of this tax-free amount, for example rent, mortgage or student fees.

> In general, employers don't want to have to pay 40 or 50 bills for you because it adds to their administration work. The arrangements are usually not a free-for-all but constrained by the employer.
>
> Ted Flack, Centre of Philanthropy and NFP Studies

In some cases, the employer provides vehicle and petrol allowances. The advantage of such benefits is that they effectively reduce the cost of living. Such benefits help to make NFP incomes quite competitive with some profit sector jobs.

Who are the main employers?

'Not-for-profit' is an umbrella term that is used to refer to any and every organsiation that is working to improve the planet or living standards, regardless of size, capacity and comparative success. This includes not only health and welfare, the environment, wildlife and sustainable development, but also advocacy groups such as Australians for Native Title and Reconcilliation and the Refugee Council of Australia. Then there are the hundreds of thousands of NFP sporting, community and arts organisations.

Since this book focuses on NFPs that are helping to make the world a better place, people interviewed come from a number of different fields:

- health and social services

- environmental

- social justice and political advocacy

- aid and relief

- animal welfare

- government-sponsored organisations.

Keep in mind, though, that many of these organisations could fit into more than one category – for example, the Australian Koala Foundation is both an animal welfare group and an environmental group that is concerned with preserving Australia's wildlife. Similarly, Médecins Sans Frontières is a medical organisation that provides both health care and international aid at the same time.

Health and social services

The combined area of health and social services, according to the NFP Roundtable figures, makes up a massive 41 per cent of the NFP sector. Here are some organisations you may be familiar with.

detour

Find out about other health jobs in Career FAQs *Medicine, Nursing* and *Allied Health.*

www.careerfaqs.com.au

- Anglicare
- Australian Red Cross
- Barnardos
- Brotherhood of St Laurence
- Cancer Council Australia
- Care
- Care Australia
- Diabetes Australia
- Exodus Foundation
- Jesuit Social Services
- Leukaemia Foundation

- Mission Australia
- MS Society
- National Heart Foundation
- Red Cross
- Royal Flying Doctor Service
- Salvation Army
- Smith Family
- St Vincent de Paul Society
- Vision Australia
- Youth off the Streets

There are also the many religious organisations, hospitals, state-based cancer councils, institutes of medical and welfare research and so forth that are NFP organisations in this sector.

Environment

Environmental groups include those that focus on the protection of the planet – its wildlife and sustainability. Others work for the protection and preservation of heritage sites. Here's just a few of them.

- Australian Conservation Foundation

- Australian Rainforest Conservation Society

- Greenpeace

- Landcare Australia

- National Trust

- Waterwatch Australia

- The Wilderness Society

Many environmental organisations rely on raising money from the public to keep their work going. Some are Australian focused while others have a global agenda – Greenpeace, for example, is an international organisation with branches all over the world.

Social justice and political advocacy

Many groups form to provide a voice for different sectors of the community. Their main role is to increase awareness of the cause and to change public opinion or government policy in some cases. The following examples of advocacy organisations show the diversity of their core business.

- Australian Council of Social Services (ACOSS)
- Australians for Native Title and Reconciliation (ANTAR)
- Refugee Council of Australia (RCOA)
- Women's Electoral Lobby (WEL).

Since the rise and rise of the Internet, many advocacy groups utilise the electronic media to raise awareness. The website GetUp, for example, allows people to join via their email or Internet connection, to receive information via email and to be actively involved in campaigns with the click of a mouse.

Aid and relief organisations

The work of aid organisations came sharply into focus after the Boxing Day Tsunami of 2004. The overwhelming support that flowed to many organisations following that disaster, and the work they carried out in the devastated regions, highlighted the exemplary work of such charities. Here are just some of the organisations that have offices in Australia.

- CARE Australia
- Fred Hollows Foundation
- Médecins Sans Frontières
- Oxfam Australia
- World Vision

There is obviously a strong need for these organisations to respond to specific crises – which they do – but they also provide support and relief all the year round.

GetUp has a board that includes community organiser Amanda Tattersall, union leader Bill Shorten, Green activist Cate Faehrmann, and technology entrepreneur Evan Thornley. It's executive director, Brett Solomon, founded and coordinated the International Youth Parliament with Oxfam, has worked for Amnesty Internaional Australia and consulted to Focus on the Global South.

Animal welfare

Whether saving an animal in the wild, looking after the health and welfare of pets or making sure farm animals are treated with care and compassion, there is an animal rights or welfare group to do the job. You will probably recognise some of the following organisations.

detour

If you love animals and would love a job working with them, find out about the many opportunities to do so in Career FAQs *Working with Animals*, coming soon!

www.careerfaqs.com.au

- Animal Welfare League

- Australian Koala Foundation

- RSPCA

- World Wildlife Fund

For people who love animals and want to match their career to that passion, these organisations can help people do just that.

Government sponsored organisations

In addition to the many different not-for-profit charities and aid organisations, there are opportunities to help others by becoming involved in government-funded volunteer work. Young Australians (between 18 and 30) can have the opportunity to become overseas development volunteers through the Australian Youth Ambassadors for Development (AYAD) Program. There's also VIDA (Volunteering for International Development from Australia), an organisation that allows people of all ages to work as volunteers in developing countries.

Many volunteers, particularly through the AYAD program, have also found ongoing work made available for them upon their return to Australia – so it really is a smart career move! If you have skills in nursing, human resources, IT, engineering, building and construction, education – just about anything really – you can put them to good use in the Asia-Pacific region through government-sponsored volunteer work.

What are employers looking for?

So, it's personally fulfilling, rewarding and truly satisfying to work in an NFP – but does everyone have what it takes? Most employers stress that despite all it's benefits, charitable work is not the kind of path that you can stroll down – it really is hard work and very draining!

You need more than just fire in your belly – you need to be resilient, thick skinned, flexible, adaptable, determined and innovative. And on top of that – you need to be qualified! Employers want to see demonstrable skills sets and also want to see that you've reaped the benefits of past experience. As always, the best way to find out what employers want is to ask them – so we've done it for you!

Meet some employers

We interviewed three employers from different NFP organisations in Australia so that they can give you some insight into their corner of the sector, and what gets them excited as an employer.

- Deborah Tabart – CEO, Australian Koala Foundation
- Sam Broughton – Fundraising manager, Salvation Army
- Trish McDonald – HR officer, CARE Australia

Deborah Tabart – CEO, Australian Koala Foundation

Deborah has been fundraising since 1969 when she helped raise funds for cerebral palsy during her time as a Miss Australia entrant. She has since worked with a number of different charities here and overseas, raising money for retarded children, lepers, Vietnamese refugees and cancer research. She has been CEO of the Australian Koala Foundation since 1988 and is often referred to as the 'koala woman'.

What are you looking for in prospective employees?
Many people think that saving the koala will be easy, and that working with them is all cuteness and cuddles. However, working for a research organisation that also has environmental credentials can be very difficult.

You need great resilience to deal with the knockbacks that invariably occur when you ask for money and don't get it. I have found that a persistent personality is essential, particularly in PR, marketing and fundraising. I think it is great to have university skills, particularly writing skills, but often a fundraiser is born rather than taught. Fundraisers need to have that skilful eye – one that says, I can make a dollar out of that.

What personal attributes are best suited to working in an NFP?

Resilience, determination and a thick skin are important attributes, as is vision, creativity and innovation. The ability to make something out of nothing and to discover new ways of doing things is a big asset.

How do you recruit people?

They often find us. We have used recruitment companies and invariably those people let us down. On paper they look great, but they never last the distance. Most of our staff started as volunteers because they wanted to be here and then we couldn't live without them.

What do you expect from them in terms of applications and interviews?

They need to know about what we do. I like it when they have looked at the web and can speak our language. I like it when they have a couple of ideas that they think might work. I will put any application in the bin if they have spelt my name incorrectly, or if they have written 'Dear Sir'.

What types of jobs are in demand? Are there any skill shortages in your sector?

Fundraising is by far the most important skill needed and I think good fundraisers are sadly lacking. Marketing and public relations experts are also in demand.

What particular skills are you most interested in for your organisation?

We are currently after a legal assistant, but generally speaking I'm always on the lookout for a person with innovative fundraising ideas. We're also always in need of people who can market our skills for profit – for instance, we have scientists who earn consulting wages but they don't always have the skills to promote their discoveries.

What's it like being the female head of an organisation?

I personally have worked very hard to make it an equitable workplace. I feel we are quite genderless – the men here are quite comfortable having a female boss. Because they care for koalas, I think of them as genuine and compassionate men. The women, I hope, love having a female boss – it means they're respected for their skills. My experience is that there are a lot of women working in charities but very few running them.

What can young people do to break into this industry?

Identify where you want to work and volunteer. Make yourself indispensable to the organisation.

What are the best aspects of working for an NFP organisation?

Having had the opportunity to start one from scratch, I think the best thing is our freedom to bring our skills to a cause that we all hold dear to our hearts. You can't really work for a conservation organisation if you don't love the environment. I think that applies to all charities – you have to have empathy for your cause. If you have that, then you can make a difference every day.

What are the negatives?

I have worked for some charities that were absolutely ghastly. I was sacked from one because I was too outspoken. I think there is a tremendous boys club out there running them and that many women are just spat out of the system.

Another negative is seeing things that are sad – koalas being killed, people dying of cancer, and not being able to fix the problem. Our chairman constantly asks us to evaluate whether or not we are actually making a difference. In fact, the environment is probably in a worse state now than it was when I got my job, yet I still feel that we are making a difference.

What's the difference between working in the NFP sector and working in the private or public sector?

I think people don't take us seriously sometimes – they act like it's not a real job and one day you'll wake up and have to work in the real world. I think there are many people who envy our jobs because they find their workplaces cold and they do not necessarily identify with their company's vision – how can you believe in bank profit, for instance?

Little changes make
a BIG difference.

Sam Broughton – Fundraising manager, Salvation Army

Sam has spent all his life working as a fundraiser in the NFP sector. The organisations he has helped include Red Cross, Surf Life Saving Victoria, Microsurgery Foundation and Childhood Cancer Association. Now 59, Sam says one of the best things about a career in this sector is that age is no barrier.

q&a

What are you looking for when you employ people in an NFP organisation?

You look for flexibility, you look for adaptability, you look for competencies.

One of the things with the NFP sector is that there aren't huge resources available. Many NFPs get along on the smell of an oily rag. That's not the case here at the Salvation Army – we have huge resources. But in most NFPs, budgets are tight so you need have to have a person who can work in that environment.

What personal attributes are best suited to working in an NFP organisation?

It always helps if you have an interest in the cause that you are working for. The most motivated people are those working for organisations that they truly believe in. There are NFP people who move from organisation to organisation, but the really successful ones are those who believe in the cause for which they are working. They tend to stay there a long time.

For example, I wouldn't work successfully in an animal welfare organisation because I am not rapt in animals, whereas I would work well in a human-orientated organisation.

How do you recruit people?

There's a whole range of ways. We tend to go through industry-based employment services. For example, if we're looking for a social worker, there are websites that have all the social workers. For income generation, public relations, fundraisers, we tend to go to the Fundraising Institute of Australia. Sometimes we go to external consultants.

Depending on the role, we quite often go through our church congregation. We are a member of the Christian family of churches and for some of our administration positions, we would go to our congregations and let them know we have availabilities. We also use the newspapers occasionally.

What do you expect from candidates in terms of applications and interviews?

We would ask that their application demonstrates their skills with reference to the position description. We would then call them in for an interview. We send them out information packs on the Salvation Army so they are well-briefed, but we expect them to have gone onto our internet site to see what we are about.

We have a set of standard questions that are predetermined so each candidate is asked the same question. In an interview, we would like to see adaptability, a pleasant personality, and someone prepared to continue their education. We provide our staff with ongoing education, which is usually in their own time, but we pay for it.

What types of jobs are in demand? Are there any particular skill shortages in the NFP sector?

My background has always been public relations and fundraising. I'm now nearly 60, have been employed in fundraising for 30 years and never once been unemployed. It's one sector that doesn't discriminate against age at all. In fact, it's a bonus to have experience.

There's huge demand for professional people in marketing, direct mail, public relations and fundraising. Wages are enormous these days compared with what they were two or three years ago. I think there is a demand for social workers and case workers as well.

What are the job prospects like in the NFP sector right now?

I think the job opportunities in the NFP sector are excellent; it's a growing sector. Generally the NFP sector has realised that you've got to have skilled people on board if you are going to advance – and to get skilled people on board, you have to pay them accordingly. So there are opportunities.

How do you suggest young people break people break into an NFP organisation?

Voluntary work – I started off as a volunteer for the Red Cross in Adelaide. Or do some work experience. Then depending on what area you want to work in, you can go off and do a social work degree. Or if you want to be in marketing or public relations, you get some formal qualifications in that.

What should young people know about working for an NFP organisation?

You can now feel confident that the NFP sector can be a real career choice because there are opportunities. Ten or 15 years ago it was not seen as a long-term option; it was something you did half way through your working life when you came in from the corporate sector, semi-retired. Now it's a career path.

What are the best parts of working for an NFP organisation?

It's very interesting. It's varied. If you work for an organisation you believe in, you feel like you are adding value to the community. If you're an environmentalist and you work for a conservation organisation, you get immense satisfaction from it.

What's the downside?

Many organisations don't have much money to spend so there are no flashy expense accounts. And wages are generally lower; if you are chasing the dollar alone, there are probably higher wages out in corporate sector.

What's the difference between the NFP sector and the private or public sectors?

There are cultural differences: my wife works for the Hyatt hotel chain and their culture is much stricter and more corporatised – either you follow the company line or you don't follow it at all. There's a bit more flexibility in a charity. We're not entirely motivated by the bottom line; we have other considerations. We try to break even each year – we're not necessarily aiming for a surplus. Our whole reason for being is to raise money so it can be spent out the other end, whereas in the corporate sector you are out there to please the shareholders of a company. We judge ourselves on how many people we help each year.

Is there anyone not suitable for work in this sector?

There are whole host of corporate people who try to switch across into the NFP sector who are not successful. Very few NFP people go the other way. It is a distinct skill set and an attitude set that makes people successful in this sector. I've seen many people come from a corporate background thinking it's going to be easy, but they fall on their faces for a whole bunch of reasons.

Trish McDonald – HR officer, CARE Australia

Trish has worked as a CARE recruitment officer for the last six years. During that time she has been responsible for the recruitment of staff for Australia-based positions, overseas work and emergency roles. She has also overseen recruitment for the Australian Youth Ambassador for Development Program, an AusAID initiative of which CARE Australia is a partner organisation.

Have attitudes towards the NFP sector as a legitimate career path changed?

Yes. I've been with CARE for six years and that's certainly something I have noticed. It's become far more competitive and highly skilled. I manage CARE's partnership with AusAid, Australian Youth Ambassador's Development program, and that has also become incredibly competitive. It is attracting an enormous amount of interest with people leaving uni and beginning-of-the-career-type people. They are very interested in a wide range of different projects.

What are you looking for when you employ people in an NFP organisation?

There is an emphasis on qualifications and skills. It used to be that just offering help was enough, but now there's the realisation that we need people who actually have qualifications or relevant work experience.

We look at your ability to work in teams and to lead. We need people with the right attitude who understand that we are all in this together. Language skills are needed for emergency response team members. If I have a database with people on it who speak a couple of languages, then it's a much more useful database.

Having an understanding of the relevant issues is also important. If it becomes apparent in an interview that the applicant knows their stuff, they're going to be rated highly by the interview panel.

What personal attributes are best suited to working in an NFP organisation?

The people who stay for the long haul are the ones who are interested in the ideals and share the vision of their organisation. The people who are successful candidates really care about what they are doing and want to be a small part of that overall delivery.

How do you recruit people?

We rarely use recruitment agencies. For the last six months we haven't done much press advertising. We get more response from websites. Typically I use the larger aid related websites like reliefweb (www.reliefweb.it) and alert.net (www.alertnet.org) and I also go through ACFID (Australian Council for International Development), which is the body for all of the NGOs. We also advertise on our own website.

What do you expect from candidates in terms of their applications and interviews?

We have an application form and cover letter information sheet on our website for people to fill out online or download. We prefer all of our applications to come in by email. This is an increasing trend in NFP organisations.

We request that applicants supply an up-to-date résumé, a cover sheet and a separate statement addressing the selection criteria. We require three references as well. Then we reduce the 20 or 30 applicants to a short list and let the panel make a decision.

Often we do interviews by phone because we get a lot of international applicants. Once we have done reference checks and had a final panel discussion, we would try and arrange a face-to-face meeting, whether that be with an overseas director or they may come here.

What types of jobs are in demand? Are there any skill shortages in the NFP sector, and if so what are they?

International aid is a growth area. The positions that we are struggling to fill are the Australian-based positions, which is something we have never found in the past. These positions range from HR to overseas programming.

What particular skills are you most interested in for your organisation?

www.reliefweb.it
www.alertnet.org
www.careaustralia.org
www.acfid.asn.au

People with previous HR experience and solid admin base. We also need overseas operation staff. Those are the people who are based in our head office but work directly with the program of a particular country office. They are usually the program management roles that usually progress to go into country office positions. They don't need actual aid experience but they do need project management experience and a good understanding of aid work.

If people want to work for an NFP organisation, how do you suggest they break in?

The best thing is volunteering because the skill set that we require is not the business type of project management, and you can get the skill set best by doing volunteering in an overseas office or even an Australian-based office.

There are many positions that hang off the individual projects and programs overseas. Often people may have got into a position through word-of-mouth referral or have been in a country at the time and made contact with a local or international NGO, and they have been able to provide them with some assistance for a few months or up to a year. That is invaluable for their development.

What do you feel young people should know about working for an NFP?

I would hope that they do consider it. If you have wonderful skills and qualifications, then don't knock NFPs out of your aspirations because the better skilled those organisations can be, the better they will be in doing their job.

What are some of the best aspects of working for an NFP?

Being part of the end result, whether it be alleviating poverty or supporting people, like in our case, or working for the environment.

What are the negatives?

Because we are charity based, you are always very aware of the responsibility of doing the right thing. You have to be very careful and be very aware of what you can do. We don't have a large bucket of money; we are very dependent on public support.

What are the main differences between working in the NFP sector and working in the private or public sector?

There is a cultural difference. I worked for 11 years in public service before I came here. I think there is more recognition and more respect for people and for the work you are doing, regardless of what level you are. It is much more inclusive. Staff members are asked to participate and give feedback in all decisions and we are all kept informed. It is desirable to our board and CEO that we do give feedback and that we do have opinions and bring our concerns to them.

Do you know of a myth concerning the NFP sector? What is the reality in your opinion?

When people's awareness is heightened and they become emotionally engaged when there is an emergency on, they just want to help and that's fantastic. But they are not going to be of assistance if they have nothing to offer in terms of employment. It's not just about, 'I want to help'. They are better off helping another way instead of expecting that we will deploy them to a country somewhere in the world without previous experience in this area or particular skills.

Expand your horizons...

AUSTRALIAN
youth
AMBASSADORS
for development

Skills Share • Institutional Strengthening • Sustainable Development

Use your skills to help make a difference.

Australian Youth Ambassadors for Development make a difference to the lives of thousands of individuals across the Asia-Pacific region.

The Program offers young Australians (aged 18 - 30) the chance to utilise their skills on short-term volunteer assignments overseas, and make a real contribution to development. In-country support and a living allowance are provided.

Whether you have a university background or valuable trade skills the opportunity to expand your horizons is available now.

Education • Environment • Gender • Governance • Health • Infastructure

www.ausaid.gov.au/youtham

Check the website for assignments.

Freecall (Australia) 1800 225 592

The Australian Youth Ambassadors for Development Program is an Australian Government initiative funded through the Australian-Agency for International Development.

AUSTRALIAN
youth
AMBASSADORS
for development

Managed by Austraining International

Australian Government

AusAID

SEEK.COM.AU
OPPORTUNITY

Finding the right job is a matter of exploring all the options.
And no one can provide you with more job options than **SEEK**,
Australia's number 1 job site. **SEEK** and you shall find.

Our Vision
your
Development!

World Vision

World Vision Australia offers Graduates a world of opportunities. Learning from dedicated professionals in a high profile organisation, you will measure your success through your personal and professional development as well as in the contribution you make to developing countries. Where else could you achieve this?

Do you want to work for Australias largest overseas aid and humanitarian organisation?

Areas of employment at World Vision:

- International Development
- Marketing & Public Affairs
- Accounting & Finance

- Information Technology
- Human Recources
- *Plus many more...*

Want to know the types of jobs you can do at World Vision Australia with your degree? Visit **worldvision.com.au**

VIDA
volunteering
for international
development
from australia

Want to make a difference?

Share your skills and learn new ones?

Challenge yourself in a new place and culture?

EDUCATION • ENVIRONMENT • GENDER • GOVERNANCE • HEALTH • INFRASTRUCTURE • RURAL DEVELOPMENT • TRADES

No matter what you do... whether you're an accountant, environmental scientist, lawyer, mechanic, veterinarian, nurse, social worker, teacher, engineer, researcher... there's a VIDA volunteer assignment for you.

Make a difference

VIDA places skilled Australians of all ages (18+) as volunteers in developing countries in the Asia Pacific region. VIDA Volunteers work with local counterparts to share valuable knowledge and skills that contribute to poverty reduction and the sustainable development of the communities in which they work. Volunteer assignments range from 1 month to 3 years in length.

We'll support you

VIDA provides volunteers with airfares, living and accommodation allowance, medicals, comprehensive insurance, predeparture training and in-country support. So all you'll need to bring are your skills, energy and enthusiasm.

Check the website for assignments

Freecall: 1800 995 536

www.vidavolunteers.com.au

Managed by,

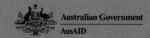 Australian Government
AusAID

 Austraining
International

 care

Insider info

What jobs could I do?

The range of 'save the world' jobs you can do are as varied as the NFP organisations you can work in.

Here is a taste of jobs you might want to consider.

- Youth support worker, Live 'N' Learn Foundation

- Communications officer, Cancer Council WA

- Captain Starlight, Children's Starlight Foundation

- Advocacy and projects funding officer, UNICEF

- Australian youth ambassador, AusAID

- Assistant country director, CARE Laos

- Fundraising and marketing officer, Australian Koala Foundation

- Graphic designer/brand coordinator, Northcott

- President, Engineers without Borders

- Project manager, AYAD

- Nutritionist, National Heart Foundation

- Actions unit manager, Greenpeace

- Campaigner coordinator, Amnesty International

- Internal audit manager, World Vision Australia

- Support services coordinator, Leukaemia Foundation

- National web manager, Wilderness Society

- HIV/AIDS and development consultant, Switzerland

- Chief pilot, Royal Australian Doctor Service

- Director, Western Australian Medical Research Institute

What do real people say about their jobs?

Silvia Ruggeri – Youth support worker, Live 'N' Learn Foundation

 cook >> waitress >> youth worker >> youth support worker

21-year-old Silvia always wanted to do something related to youth work; during her high school years she was involved in peer support programs and youth support networking. She has been working in the social welfare area for the last two years and has held her current job for four months.

Live 'N' Learn is an incentive of the NSW Department of Housing, providing safe and affordable housing for students and promoting further education.

What does your job involve?

I do case management, which involves working on a day-to-day basis with clients, dealing with issues that might come up, making phone calls on their behalf – maybe finding them a school or a traineeship or work – and finding other support networks for them, like counselling and health services.

What's your work like?

I work in a team of four – there's one manager, two youth support workers and a co-coordinator of another program. We discuss issues as a group, whether it be in the form of a debriefing, a brainstorming session or a staff meeting. My job involves doing referral and background checks, meeting with clients and staff, keeping in touch with referral agencies and reviewing the program.

How would you describe your workplace culture?

I find it's a very supportive environment; you have your manager on board and you can talk to him or her. On the downside, there are problems with resources and finances, which can make things difficult.

What do you like most about your job?

Being able to interact with different kinds of people, including clients, colleagues and people from different support agencies.

What do you like least?

When things don't go to plan for a client.

What interesting project have you been involved in?

I developed a high school program for young girls who were bullying or being bullied. The school identified the students who were at risk and we just sat and talked as a group about things like sexual health and education, and whatever other issues were raised. The group was a mixture of the bullies and those who were being bullied, the good and the bad kids – which meant that different kinds of people interacted in a way they never had before.

What do you wish someone had told you before you started on this career path?

You need a lot of time management and juggling skills.

How does your job allow you to achieve the life–work balance that suits you?

If I'm run off my feet and won't be able to finish something on a given day, I'm able to pass it on to a colleague and vice versa. Also, because we're not a 24-hour service (as many youth support services are), I do mainly day work.

What are your ambitions? Where to from here?

In a few years' time I would like to go back to university and get a degree in psychology or social work.

How necessary were your qualifications for this job?

Very necessary. And also very useful – I found that at TAFE you learn a lot from the teachers because they're actually working in the industry themselves, so they're able to share their insights and inside stories with you.

The diploma gave me the foundation; I have learnt patience and case management on the job.

What advice would you give young people looking to get into this field?

In terms of career choice, you need to be sure that this is what you want to do. Young people are already up and down themselves, so they don't want their workers to be flaky as well.

In practical terms, it's good to know someone in the sector because they can put your name out there – that's how I've gotten a lot of my positions. Work experience through TAFE is helpful, and volunteering is another way you can get your name and face known.

What did you say or do at your interview that helped you get the job?

I knew the manager here, so that made things easier for me – but it also helped that I outlined my skills clearly and talked about successful projects, like the high school bullies program.

What personal attributes best suit your job?

You have to be patient, calm, friendly and easy to talk to – young people need to feel comfortable sitting down with you for a chat.

in
brief

Youth support worker

$$$	33–35K
quals	Dip Youth Work, Campbelltown TAFE
hrs/wk	35
life–work	leave work at work
flexibility	10/10

Zoe Rudder – Communications officer, Cancer Council WA

CV shop assistant, London >> communications officer

Zoe, in her early 20s, has only been in her current job for five months but says she would never have imagined she could care so much about a workplace. She also loves the flexibility of working part time, as it allows her to pursue her freelance journalism career.

The Cancer Council WA has been Western Australia's leading cancer support organisation for 40 years. It relies predominantly on donations and volunteer helpers to provide community support, health care and education for sufferers and their families.

What do you do in your current job?

I am developing a CD library for cancer patients and I also help with media-related issues such as organising stories for newspapers.

What motivated you to choose the NFP sector?

I really loved the idea of having a career in the media that still allowed me to contribute to society. I believe very strongly in this organisation and the role it plays. I felt that this particular position would give me the chance to develop public relations as well as journalism skills.

What's your working environment like?

It's just me and one other person in the media department here, but we are situated within a larger team and everyone's always willing to help out.

What's the workplace culture like? Do you think it's different for an NFP?

It's so different! For a start, the CCWA cares about people, not just budgets – so that makes a refreshing change from retail. It's also a very supportive environment; you feel that if you had any problems, you could ask for help.

Everyone who works here does it because they really enjoy it, which means there's a great level of commitment to the job. There's also a greater degree of job satisfaction than in many other workplaces because you know that you're helping to make a difference.

What do you like most about your job?

Working with a great team of people and knowing we are having a positive impact on the lives of so many others. I never really imagined that I could care for a workplace so much.

What do you like least?

The fact that you're working for a charity means you put a lot of pressure on yourself to perform at a consistently high standard.

What's the most interesting project you've been involved in?

The CD project has been very interesting. I've had the chance to interview people who have cancer – or have beaten it – and their strength is inspiring. It helps puts your own life into perspective.

How flexible are your work arrangements?

It's very flexible – there have been a few occasions where I've had to work from home and it's never been a problem. Also, I like that I can choose to come in early and beat the traffic on the way home.

I am also a freelance journalist, so working three days a week allows me to develop that side of my career at the same time.

On the whole I feel that the CCWA is very aware that its employees are people, not robots. A lot of companies don't seem to get that.

What are your ambitions? Where to from here?

I enjoy working here so much that I can't see myself considering moving on any time soon. My ambition is to stay within the company and gain greater responsibilities.

Are your qualifications necessary in your current job?

My journalism degree has been invaluable. Not everyone is confident enough to cold call strangers and interview them – I know I wasn't before I did my degree. Also, journalism and PR have a totally

different style of writing to anything else, and that's something that really needs to be learnt. Uni was also useful in that I made the connections there that secured me both my job at the CCWA and also my job as a freelance journalist.

What did you say or do at your interview that helped you get the job?

I badly wanted the job and I think they could see that. I tried to be myself but to be professional at the same time. I felt confident that I was the right person for the job, so I tried to convey that.

What personal attributes do you think best suit your job?

I consider myself an approachable, confident person and that really helps when dealing with others. You have to make sure people will feel comfortable with you. It's also important to be confident in yourself and your abilities.

For people who want to work in the NFP sector in general, you need to care. NFP organisations rely on charity – so how can you expect other people to care if you don't yourself?

What advice would you give young people considering a career in the NFP sector?

If you feel that it's something you really want to do, go for it! The world can always do with more people who are driven to make a difference and contribute to society.

in
brief

Communications officer

$$$	I'm happy!
quals	BA Journalism, Curtin University
hrs/wk	24
life–work	good balance
flexibility	9/10

my**day**

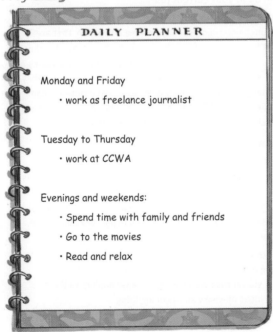

DAILY PLANNER

Monday and Friday
- work as freelance journalist

Tuesday to Thursday
- work at CCWA

Evenings and weekends:
- Spend time with family and friends
- Go to the movies
- Read and relax

find out
more

www.cancerwa.asn.au

Save the World

CV production assistant
>> media assistant >>
festival coordinator >>
information services officer
>> Captain Starlight

Marianne Randall – Captain Starlight, Starlight Children's Foundation Australia

Marianne loves the uniqueness of her job, which combines entertainment and working with children for a good cause. And while the job can sometimes be emotionally draining, the family-like atmosphere of the organisation means that everybody tends to support each other.

The Starlight Children's Foundation aims to brighten the lives of hospitalised children through programs such as Starlight Escapes, which send sick children and their families on holiday together, and Starlight Wishgranting. The foundation has the support of healthcare professionals, sports and entertainment personalities, business people and large corporations like Qantas.

What do you do in your current job?

The role of a Captain Starlight is to help brighten the lives of seriously ill children through entertainment and positive distraction. I'm based in the Sydney Children's Hospital at Randwick. I run a room called the Starlight Express, which is full of entertainment, activities and games for the kids. There are Nintendos and a stage for performers when they come in – we run game shows everyday. We also host a closed circuit TV channel called Starlight TV, which runs 24 hours a day, seven days a week. Then there's Starlight Radio, which runs four days a week.

What's your workplace culture like?

We have a really great cohesive team of captains. We're very much a team. Because we have to rely on donated goods and services, there is a need to share contacts, information and ideas. There's also a sense of being willing to put in extra time, even when you know that you're not going to get paid for it. It feels almost like you're part of a family here, since we all touch base daily and share stories about the kids.

On the negative side, you are often expected to go the extra mile without getting too many perks for your efforts. Also, sometimes things happen slower than we'd like because we don't have the budget for big ideas or wacky shows or anything.

Do you think the workplace culture of the private sector differs from NFP organisations?

I used to work for Getty Images and I think people were more isolated in their jobs there. There wasn't such a holistic sense of what people were moving towards; it was more about selling things and making money.

What do you like most about your job?

The creative freedom, and being able to work with kids.

What do you like least?

It's very draining – you experience such extremes in emotions. That can be very challenging.

What's the most interesting project you've been involved in?

I would say that working on Starlight TV is always interesting! We're always on the lookout for things that we can use to keep things lively, like interactive game shows and stuff like that. We do everything ourselves. For example, we made a CD of songs about Planet Starlight – which is where we're supposedly from – and we've used it to structure the TV program.

What do you wish someone had told you before you started in this career?

That you don't earn a lot of money. But that's never been a huge drive for me. I've never looked at my career like that. It's addictive; it can be hard to leave once you get in.

How does your job allow you to achieve the life–work balance that suits you?

It can be very flexible here when you need time off to do other things. In theory it's a nine-to-five job but things can be shifted about if necessary. We're encouraged to do professional development and training that will improve our skills, whether it's entertainment based or counselling and psychology-type stuff. We can also get time in lieu if we have to work overtime.

What are your ambitions?

My experiences here have showed me that I enjoy entertaining and being creative, so I'd like to go into perhaps film or television. But I would still like to keep some aspects of the NFP sector alive in my career – I want to feel that I'm working towards something meaningful.

Have your qualifications been necessary for your job?

My qualifications are not totally necessary, but they have been beneficial since I'm running a closed circuit TV show. I also studied some music, which has helped. All the captains have different backgrounds, but experience in children's entertainment was a necessary element for getting the job.

There are other skills that I've developed through on-the-job experience, such as learning how to use different equipment, as well as different performance and media skills.

What did you say or do at your interview that helped you get the job?

I think having a positive attitude was something that helped me. Applicants also have to do a little audition piece, and mine was a musical performance. I talked a lot about my experience in performing, which is very varied: I've done circus, theatre and party entertainment for kids. I was just really open and honest – and I had a sense of humour.

What personal attributes do you think best suit your job?

People skills are the most important. I have to be able to relate to anyone from a four-year-old to a corporate businessperson who wants to donate money. So communication skills are vital, as is emotional intelligence and a sense of fun.

What characteristics are best suited to NFP work?

Openness. Empathy. Good communication. Innovation is also important because you can't always do things the normal way. And you need to be able to work with a lot of different personalities.

in
brief

Captain Starlight	
$$$	40K
quals	BA Media, Macquarie University
hrs/wk	40
life–work	I make sure to look after myself
flexibility	8.5/10

my**day**

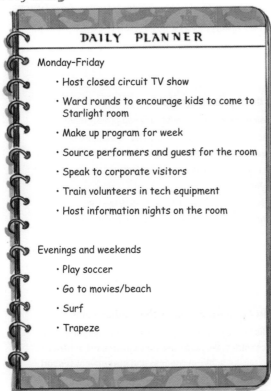

DAILY PLANNER

Monday-Friday

- Host closed circuit TV show
- Ward rounds to encourage kids to come to Starlight room
- Make up program for week
- Source performers and guest for the room
- Speak to corporate visitors
- Train volunteers in tech equipment
- Host information nights on the room

Evenings and weekends

- Play soccer
- Go to movies/beach
- Surf
- Trapeze

find out
more

www.starlight.org.au

Felicity Stafford – Advocacy and projects funding officer, UNICEF Australia

 Felicity first considered working in the NFP sector while on exchange in Chile – she says that seeing the good work UNICEF was doing there made her want to contribute. After doing volunteer work and another overseas stint in Fiji as part of the AYAD (Australian Youth Ambassador for Development) program, she landed a full-time job at UNICEF Australia.

UNICEF is the United Nations Children's Fund. Its Australian mission is to raise awareness and funds for UNICEF's work in the field which covers 155 countries and territories. The fund aims to help children overcome poverty, abuse and disease by providing education, health care, clean water and basic community infrastructure. UNICEF Australia also assists Indigenous communities in Central Australia.

q&a

What do you do in your current job?

These are two sides to my work – advocacy and project funding.

The project funding element refers to seeking funding for our children's projects in the Asia Pacific region and in central Australia. At the moment I'm mainly involved with projects in Vanuatu, Fiji and the Solomon Islands.

The advocacy element is diverse. I'm involved in the **CRC** taskforce, which is a group of child's rights-based agencies working to ensure that all children in Australia are protected and their rights respected. It's my job to try and mobilise public awareness on various campaigns, such as UNICEF's five-year HIV and AIDs campaign. I also work closely with our partner organisation, AYAD, facilitating placements and prepping them before they leave.

Who runs UNICEF and where does the funding come from?

UNICEF Australia is one of 37 national committees operating in industrialised countries. We help raise funds in support of UNICEF's work while also raising public awareness and government support for the welfare of vulnerable women and children. UNICEF's national committees raise nearly one third of the fund's global income through fundraising campaigns, corporate partnerships, government assistance and the sale of cards and gifts.

What motivated you to work in the NFP sector?

It wasn't something I always intended but more of a process that developed when I started traveling. As part of my double degree I studied in Chile for a year. While I was over there I got involved in a couple of voluntary community organisations. I did some work with kids, got into fundraising and met some great people along the way.

When I came back to Australia and finished university I got a job at another NFP organisation that runs educational programs including language classes, cultural exchange and study tours you can undertake overseas to learn on the ground rather than just learning in the classroom.

That's where it all started – I knew that from then on I wanted to work in the NFP sector. So I applied to AYAD and went to Fiji for 12 months, and haven't really looked back.

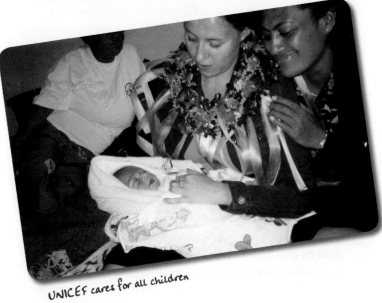

UNICEF cares for all children

What did you do in Fiji?

I was in Fiji through AusAID's AYAD program. AusAID is the Australian government agency responsible for managing Australia's overseas aid program. I was working with Habitat for Humanity, an international NFP organisation that basically helps build houses for low-income families.

My role was Resource Development and Communications Manager. In my job I developed proposals and sought funding from the private sector and from international governments – primarily Australia, New Zealand and Canada. I did other communication and marketing activities, including organising events, producing a quarterly newsletter and a lot of PR work. I also went out into the villages to speak to women talk about their lives and the struggle that they faced. We would use the stories we collected in our funding proposals.

We also got involved in actually building some of the houses. With all the international volunteers, the houses would go up in two weeks – very simple ones obviously, but they had walls and a kitchen and a bathroom that the family would otherwise never have had. It was great being in the village and really being involved with the local people and seeing what a difference it makes to their lives.

What did you do when you came back to Australia?

I started volunteering at UNICEF Australia while I was looking for work. Then I got an AYAD internship in which AusAID provides funding for 20 days of work in the development sector. I was given a project to do – a situation analysis for UNICEF Australia's HIV and AIDS campaign. This involved developing a strategy for how UNICEF Australia could potentially support the HIV/AIDS events happening in Australia. After that 20-day period, which I did part time over two months, they offered me a full-time job.

How many people work at UNICEF Australia?

There are around 25 full-time staff and a couple of part-time staff, and then quite a number of volunteers who come in periodically as well.

Have you travelled much in this job?

No – I've only been in the job for five months. But there is talk about it in the future. I was supposed to go to Timor just before the recent crisis, but that was cancelled.

What do you like most about your job?

I love that it's just so diverse. Every day is different. I love being involved in overseas projects and knowing thing are happening internationally. I'm also enjoying being involved in raising public awareness and helping other people go out and help make a difference.

What do you like least?

For many NFPs, limited funding is an issue and we're not as well-resourced as we'd like to be. There's a lot of work to be done and there aren't enough hours in the day to get it done. But the assistance of volunteers makes a huge difference to get through the workload – we wouldn't be able to do what we do without volunteers.

Do you have to do volunteer work before you can get a paid job in this sector?

You need to have done some volunteer work so that you understand the aims and structure of the industry and the type of work that's involved. Judging from the number of volunteers coming through who are very well educated, and have brilliant work experience and skills, I'd say the more experience you have, the better. Getting involved and doing some volunteer work either here or internationally is a real bonus and something people should think about doing.

detour

Find out more about overseas jobs in Career FAQs *Going Global*

www.careerfaqs.com.au

What do you wish someone had told you about this sector before you started out?

Be flexible, be prepared for the unexpected. In UNICEF emergency situations happen and you really have to hit the ground running.

Does your job provide a good life–work balance that suits you?

Yes, definitely. My official hours are 9.00 am to 5.30 pm; we sometimes stay back till 6.30 or 7.00, but not often later than that. I have my weekends free. I'm happy with it.

What qualifications are necessary to work in this field?

The qualifications depend on the actual job you want to do. There are some very useful degrees – social sciences, international or social development, project management, PR, marketing, media and communications, finance or HR, depending on the job you're aiming for.

Where would you like to go from here?

I'd love to have the opportunity to work overseas again – Asia, South America or maybe Africa.

What's a typical income in your job?

Around $40 000. Working in charities you also get tax benefits, meaning that a percentage of your salary is not taxed – but the actual percentage depends on the organisation. It's called 'reportable fringe benefits'. At UNICEF Australia our RFB is 30 per cent.

find out
more

ACFID
www.acfid.asn.au

AusAID
www.ausaid.gov.au

UNICEF Australia
www.unicef.org.au

What did you say or do at your interview that helped you get the job?

I guess I demonstrated an understanding of development issues and UNICEF thematic areas. And my previous experience in volunteer work would have helped – I think that shows that you're dedicated and willing to go the extra mile.

Where should young people start looking for an NFP job?

The ACFID (Australian Council for International Development) website advertises all sorts of development jobs. That's one of the best places to start. And if you look at the AusAID website they also have a list of all the NGOs in Australia. Then there's seek.com and other job search websites – we advertise on all of them as well.

ⁱⁿ
brief

Advocacy and projects
funding officer

$$$ 45K

quals   BA International
         Studies, B
         Business, UTS

hrs/wk   40+

life–work I'm happy with it

flexibility good

my**week**

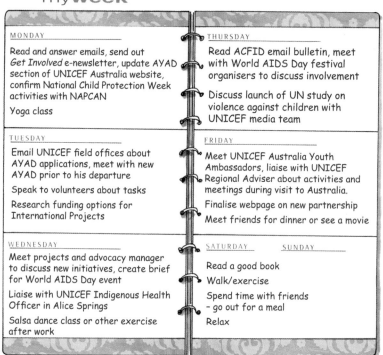

MONDAY	THURSDAY
Read and answer emails, send out *Get Involved* e-newsletter, update AYAD section of UNICEF Australia website, confirm National Child Protection Week activities with NAPCAN Yoga class	Read ACFID email bulletin, meet with World AIDS Day festival organisers to discuss involvement Discuss launch of UN study on violence against children with UNICEF media team
TUESDAY	FRIDAY
Email UNICEF field offices about AYAD applications, meet with new AYAD prior to his departure Speak to volunteers about tasks Research funding options for International Projects	Meet UNICEF Australia Youth Ambassadors, liaise with UNICEF Regional Adviser about activities and meetings during visit to Australia. Finalise webpage on new partnership Meet friends for dinner or see a movie
WEDNESDAY	SATURDAY SUNDAY
Meet projects and advocacy manager to discuss new initiatives, create brief for World AIDS Day event Liaise with UNICEF Indigenous Health Officer in Alice Springs Salsa dance class or other exercise after work	Read a good book Walk/exercise Spend time with friends – go out for a meal Relax

Alix Campbell – Australian youth ambassador, Vietnam

Alix is based in Vietnam as a construction assistant for one year as part of the Australian Youth Ambassador for Development program (AYAD). The program provides opportunities for young professionals under thirty to volunteer for projects in developing countries throughout Asia and the Pacific. The aim of the program is to facilitate the transfer of skills and strengthen mutual understanding between Australia and other Asia-Pacific countries.

CV fast food worker >> bar worker >> engineer >> Australian youth ambassador

q&a

fyi

GHD Pty Ltd is an international professional services company that employs nearly 5000 people in Australia, Asia, the USA and elsewhere. Its main function is to recruit professionals in the ares of infrastructure, mining and industry, defence, property and the environment.

How did you come to live and work in Vietnam?

I worked for an engineering company in Sydney called GHD Pty Ltd that provides engineering and project management services on AusAID projects in Asia, including Vietnam. I was offered the opportunity to apply for my AYA position by GHD – which has supplied a number of previous AYAs – then I applied to AusAID and got their support.

Where in Vietnam do you live?

I live in a town called Bac Lieu. Bac Lieu is in the Mekong Delta, a six-hour drive south of Ho Chi Minh City.

What do you do in your spare time?

I spend a lot of weekends traveling around the Mekong Delta. Once every three weeks or so I visit Ho Chi Minh City. Last weekend my friend and I drove a moto from Bac Lieu to Long Xuyen for the weekend. We spent time stopping at little roadside cafes and hired a boat to visit some wholesale floating markets in Long Xuyen.

How do you get by as a volunteer?

As part of the AYAD program, AusAID gives me a small living allowance that is enough for pre-departure medical expenses (vaccinations and the like) as well accommodation and food while I'm in the country.

What do you do in your job?

I'm involved with the Three Delta Towns (3DT) project, which provides Bac Lieu with a clean water supply and working drainage, wastewater and solid waste systems.

I assist with project management, site safety and quality assurance procedures. I visit the construction sites daily to inspect things like environment controls and safety measures. My job also requires the creation of construction schedules to assist the construction companies involved in planning their resources, and I monitor the progress of works.

What is it like living and working in another country?

Living and working in Vietnam was all a bit of a blur for the first two months. It was a crazy time for me – learning to live in Vietnam as well as starting a new job at the same time, all in a foreign language.

I have gradually acquired enough Vietnamese to get by on a day-to-day basis. I find myself learning a whole range of words. My tutor has taught me about food and traffic – my work colleagues have taught me about engineering. This means I can say the Vietnamese word for 'rice' as well as the one for 'water treatment plant'!

Working in Vietnam as a female engineer was difficult at first as I was initially assumed to be my boss's secretary, and was introduced as such in the first work meeting I attended. But I'm gradually gaining the respect of the people I am working with and I hope to be able to speak more Vietnamese soon, so that I can increase my ability to interact with them.

Are there others in the AYA program working with you?

I have a fantastic network of other AYAs who are working in Vietnam. There are nine based in Ho Chi Minh City and two in the Mekong Delta. I'm in constant contact with them – they're my new family over here.

I also work with other Australians and several Vietnamese who speak English. My current supervisor in Bac Lieu was an AYA before me and we used to work together in Sydney.

What's involved in the application process to be an AYA?

The positions for this program are advertised on the AusAID website. Intakes are made three times each year and the program is currently expanding to offer approximately 400 positions a year.

To apply for an AYA position, an extensive paperwork trail is required, including a CV, application form, passport photos, a criminal history check and three professional references. Each applicant can apply for as many positions as they wish. After the submission of an application it takes approximately three months to find out whether it's been successful or not.

After this long wait – and if you're successful – there's a heap of things to complete, such as medical checks, pre-departure training and preparation for departure, all within about two months.

What do you like most about your work?

I'm learning so much about engineering, culture and people. I like working both indoors and outdoors on a day-to-day basis. And I like seeing others learning from me.

The Australian Youth Ambassadors for Development (AYAD) Program places skilled Australians aged 18–30, on short term assignments (3–12 months in the Asia–Pacific region.

Volunteering isn't just for youth. VIDA (Volunteering for International Development from Australia) places skilled Australian volunteers of all ages throughout Asia and the Pacific. Check out www.vidavolunteers.com.au for more info.

Alix Campbell on site in Vietnam

What do you like least?

The part I like the least is the part I find the most challenging – speaking the native language. I wish I could speak it so as to gain more respect from all the Vietnamese people I meet – from the people I work with everyday to the people I drink coffee with.

What have you gained from being an AYA?

I can already tell that I will learn a lot from my year as an AYA. It's a valuable experience in tolerance, acceptance, understanding, humour, laughing, loving, challenges, innovation, support ... It's been a hard thing to do for me, living in a foreign country that doesn't have all the luxuries of home.

What's on the cards for you next?

I guess from here I will head back to Sydney for a swim at the beach, a sandwich and a coffee. After that, I'll think about which part of the water industry I want to aim for a job in. Probably something to do with sustainable water resources ... Who knows!

Nami Nelson – Assistant country director, CARE Laos

Nami's parents were both volunteers in Malaysia when they met, so you might say she didn't really have a choice about what she would end up wanting to do; it was already in her blood. It was, however, her time as an exchange student in Thailand at the age of 15 that cemented her interest in development work, which she has been involved in for the last four years. She has been in her current job for three months.

CARE Australia is currently one of the most prominent humanitarian organisations, supplying aid and long-term development programs all over the world. It was established in 1987 by former Prime Minister Malcolm Fraser and is part of the CARE International group.

q&a

What does your job involve?

I coordinate the CARE Laos projects in reproductive health, rural development and disaster management. I am responsible for

managing staff and for ensuring the accurate and effective design, implementation and evaluation of CARE Laos projects. This involves working closely with project staff, on-the-job mentoring and supervision, conducting workshops and travelling around the country to various project sites.

How did you get into this kind of work?

I did some research on HIV and AIDS in Vietnam while I was studying there, and later in Thailand as part of my honours year. At that point I started looking at how I could get more involved in HIV/AIDS-related work, and I saw an Australian Youth Ambassador position advertised for an HIV program on the Thai-Cambodian border. I didn't speak Khmer, but I do speak Thai, which I thought could be useful.

Festival in Vientiane, Laos

What's the most interesting project you've been involved in?

Our reproductive health project in Vientiane has been really moving and rewarding. We train young locals as peer educators to help inform their friends and co-workers about HIV/AIDS and sexual health. At night we go with them to discos and bars as young girls are preparing for their night's work, and hold discussions about various topics including how to protect yourself from HIV and **STI**s.

The peer educators – many of them ex- or current bar girls themselves – have developed a short play based on real events in which a young girl drinks a little too much, is raped by a man she trusts, attempts an abortion that goes very wrong, and ends up requiring serious medical care and unable to have children.

glossary

STI means:

– sexually-transmitted infection.

Watching the audience is as moving as the story itself. The girls are all riveted, and when it comes time to discuss contraceptive methods and other things, they're all keen to be involved.

What kind of difficulties are involved with working in a foreign country?

Cultural differences are a major issue when it comes to working overseas. Although I have lived, studied and worked in Asia for much of the last 10 years, there will always be things to learn. It's important to remain open and listen to other people's perspectives, and keep in mind that my way is not necessarily always the best way.

Personal safety in terms of driving skills is definitely something that you need to adjust your mind to. Traffic here is like a school of fish – sudden movement can disrupt the whole flow and cause chaos! It's pretty intimidating at first to step out onto a road with traffic flying about in what seems like no order at all, but after a while you begin to get the feel for how things do work and you adapt accordingly.

Another issue of personal safety is about trusting the planes you have to fly in, which are possibly maintained at slightly less than the standard you would expect at home!

MYTH

overseas assignments are all about bludging in the tropics

fact

Being posted overseas is hard work. Learning to live and in another country and culture is fun, but can be taxing as well.

How do you cope with these difficulties?

Relearning how to calculate risks in a new context is very important. Risks do need to be taken everyday – the important thing is to make sure you're aware of them and how to reduce them.

Cultural misunderstandings will always be a part of life overseas. Learning to laugh at yourself and your mistakes, asking questions

and being responsive to the way others think and act all help to make adjusting to a new environment or cultural context easier.

What personal attributes are best suited to this kind of work?

An open mind, flexibility, willingness to go with the flow. An attitude that says nothing can faze you.

What do you like most about your work?

The people I work with – they're so talented and committed to what they're doing and why they're doing it. It might sound a bit cheesy, but it's also great when you're able to see that your team's work has made a difference in someone's life.

What do you like least?

A lot of travel is involved, which many people may think would be a wonderful thing – and of course it is, to a point – but it can also be very demanding when you're never in the same place for more than a couple of days. And it also means being away from friends and family at home!

How useful are your qualifications for your current job?

My background in Asian Studies has been very useful, especially the fact that I speak Thai, as Thai and Lao are very closely related languages.

What sort of benefits do you get with your salary?

The benefits are excellent when you're posted overseas. We get rest and recuperation entitlements, provisions for emergency evacuation if necessary, and flights to and from our assigned destinations (which also includes your spouse/partner and children if the post is designated as 'accompanied'). We also get our rent and utilities (water, gas and electricity) paid for.

find out
more

www.careaustralia.org.au

If you're employed by CARE Australia but not an Australian citizen you don't pay tax, and Australian citizens only get taxed for their first 31 days of employment.

Life–work balance – how much of a challenge is it?

It's a VERY big challenge! There's such a lot of work to do, and you feel a real sense of responsibility – not just in a professional sense but emotional and moral responsibility as well.

However, it's also important to realise that there's only so much you can do. If you work so hard that you burn out you aren't going to be working effectively for anyone. It can be hard to make time for myself when so many demands need to be met, but it also needs to be a priority.

in
brief

Assistant country director	
$$$	60–80K
quals	B Asian Studies (Hons), ANU
life–work	needs work
flexibility	6.5/10

What should young people consider before getting into this type of work?

Be honest with yourself about why you want to do it, what it takes, and your own capabilities. You need to understand that the changes you want to make are going to take longer than you might expect. It's the small changes you need to look for, not that you have changed an entire community in six months.

my**day**

DAILY PLANNER

Monday–Friday

- Review project achievements and expenditure with managers
- Recruit new staff
- Design new projects and create submissions for funding
- Liaise between the organisation and donors
- Overview program quality
- Visit project teams in the field

Evenings and weekends

- Play touch football
- Hang out with friends
- Take belly dancing class
- Read

Hannah Richardson – Fundraising and marketing officer, Australian Koala Foundation

 CV Allianz intern, Munich >> independent fundraiser >> assistant English teacher, Japan >> office manager >> fundraising and marketing officer

After raising money for Raleigh International and taking a trip to Ghana in West Africa, 27-year-old Hannah has been driven by the realisation that everyone has the potential to give something to those in need, be it time, money or just compassion. Only six months into her current job, she hopes to make a difference for a long time to come.

The Australian Koala Foundation is a non-government organisation that aims to protect koalas and their natural environment from disease and the effects of human incursion. Founded in 1986 at its Brisbane headquarters, the group focuses on research, conservation and koala education. Twenty thousand people subscribe to the magazine and website hits number one million each year.

fyi

Raleigh International is a youth development charity founded in 1978 by Prince Charles. It aims to foster self-confidence and leadership skills in young people through adventure expeditions, scientific exploration and community service.

 q&a

What do you do in your current job?

My job is to strengthening the AKF brand through marketing strategy, fundraising, sourcing merchandise for our online shop and writing proposals for sponsorship. I also assist the general manager and CEO.

What was your job before this one?

I worked for Médecins Sans Frontières as a fundraiser, but in a very different context to what I do now. Back then I was doing face-to-face fundraising, which means stopping people in the street and asking them for donations. Now my work is much more office-based.

What motivated you to work in the NFP sector?

When I was at university, I had aspirations to work in marketing for a large corporation. But my experience raising $8000 for Raleigh International – which led to an expedition to Ghana in West Africa – turned things around for me completely. I've been driven ever since by the realisation that everyone can contribute to society.

What's your work environment like?

I work in a small team, most particularly with the general manager and the PR officer.

I get on well with my CEO, who has been with the organisation since it was set up, and is always coming up with great ideas for me to work on. I also work closely with the IT and projects coordinator to strengthen the brand, as well as the administration and finance manager.

What do you like most about your job?

I love the variety. Every day there is a new challenge awaiting me. I have so many projects going on all at once. It can be quite daunting sometimes, but it is also a lot of fun and has taught me to organise myself better.

I get to meet amazing, generous, inspiring people and to feel that I'm making a difference in some small way – I'm very passionate about the environment and believe there are so many little things that people can change in their everyday lives to help save our planet. Working for an organisation like the AKF allows me to have a small voice and encourage people to act more responsibly.

MYTH

environmentalists are
all unwashed hippies

fact

We shower just like
everyone else – but
we turn off the water
while soaping ourselves
to save water!

What do you like least?

The inherent negativity involved in any fundraising: the fact that we have to fundraise for whatever given project means that there's something wrong in the world, and sometimes you feel like nothing you do will ever fix it. Plus the negativity we encounter from people who think we're raising money for our own personal gain.

What's a recent project you've been involved in?

I was involved in launching a regular e-newsletter for the staff at the AKF. It's been a really rewarding project as we've already had some very positive results and feedback.

Where do you see opportunities for growth in this sector?

Fundraising and marketing. The smaller NFP organisations don't have the budget to pay for an efficient marketing strategy, and so don't grow – it's a vicious cycle. There is potential for huge growth in public funding, but currently only a very small percentage of people actually donate. This is something that needs to change. I believe everyone can afford to give something and giving to a good cause is really empowering.

What do you wish someone had told you before you started?

That it would be a constant uphill battle. And that no matter how good the cause is, there are always people who perceive it as a waste of time and money.

How does your job allow you to achieve the life–work balance that suits you?

I love that I can bring my values to work and everyone respects them. I am not expected to do overtime and can work flexible hours. We can take leave without pay and our boss is very approachable if we have any problems at all.

What are your ambitions? Where to from here?

I would like to help the Australian Koala Foundation grow and become an even more recognisable brand worldwide. If I stay in Brisbane, I can see a long and happy career here.

in brief

Fundraising and
marketing officer

$$$ 45–70K

quals   German and
        Management
        Studies (Hons),
        Leeds Uni, UK

hrs/wk   40

life–work   better than most

flexibility   8/10

Are your qualifications necessary for your current role?

The skills I gained from my degree are definitely useful in my job. I also gained a lot of useful skills and a thick skin from my previous experience fundraising and teaching.

What did you say or do at your interview that helped you get the job?

I was very enthusiastic about animal welfare and protection. I also showed that I could be thick-skinned and not be put off by rejections, which is really important in my position.

What personal attributes do you think best suit your job?

I am always friendly and enthusiastic, even when someone isn't giving me what I'm asking for. I'm also very persistent and won't take no for an answer. I'm very passionate about all philanthropic causes and especially about our environment, so I fight hard to get what I want in this job. If I wasn't passionate about it, it would be very difficult to persuade others to be.

myday

DAILY PLANNER

Monday–Friday

- Check emails
- Write sponsorship proposals
- Brainstorm new fundraising ideas
- Source new merchandise for the online Save the Koala shop
- Meet with general manager
- Update marketing plan

Weekends

- Play touch rugby
- Go rock climbing or to the gym
- Dinner and drinks with friends
- Watch a movie

find out more

www.savethekoala.com

Nicola Sutherland – Graphic designer, Northcott Society

CV building consultancy
assistant >> waitress >>
graphic designer

Nicola, in her late 20s, has been working for Northcott for the past two years. She describes her time there as a learning curve and says that creativity and being able to think outside the square are the most important assets in her job. Since budgets for disability organisations can be tight that big glossy ad is not always possible!

Formerly known as the NSW Society for Crippled Children, Northcott provides services, support, products, and information for people with disabilities, as well as their families and carers. It aims to maximise the potential of individuals with disabilities, with over 40 programs running in NSW for people with spina bifida, cerebral palsy, muscular dystrophy and other neuro-muscular disorders.

q&a

What do you do in your current job?

I take care of all design aspects and brand coordination for Northcott, including all collateral, events and publications.

What motivated you to choose the NFP sector, and this job in particular?

I always wanted to work in this sector, but wanted to be behind the scenes. I wanted to make a difference and help people. I enjoy knowing that I'm indirectly helping to make someone's life more enjoyable.

What's your work environment like?

I work alongside the public relations coordinator, with whom I coordinate publications, newspaper articles and the like. I also work closely with the marketing director on branding and brand awareness both externally and internally.

What sort of workplace culture is specific to working in NFPs?

I think there is a really caring attitude in the NFP sector – people always make an effort to say hello and learn about each other's lives. And there's always a morning tea on for anyone who leaves! But at the same time, the people are very professional and passionate about their jobs, perhaps even more so than in the public or private sectors.

On the downside, the culture can be somewhat bureaucratic; certain work and projects can't be made public until they've been approved by a heap of different people in every nook and cranny of the organisation. Budgets can be tight, which means that glossy colour ad you've been dreaming about might have to be black and white instead.

One of Nicola's designs

What's the most interesting project you've been involved in?

I was involved in creating a theme for a cricket legends lunch, a fundraising event with some high-profile sporting legends. The theme was 10 years of Australia beating the West Indies and generally dominating cricket. The look was inspired by a cinema poster from *Gone with the Wind* – we called it Gone with the Windies!

Where do you see the opportunities for growth in this sector?

I see a major growth in aged care. People with disabilities are now living much longer. New technology such as mobility equipment is also an area that I think will grow.

What do you wish someone had told you before you started on this career path?

How difficult it is to get people to stop using out-of-date logos!

How flexible are your work arrangements?

They're very flexible – I get time in lieu, leave without pay and salary sacrifice.

Where do you see yourself in the future?

I'd like to stay in the NFP sector for a while longer; it's interesting learning about other aspects of life. I would also like to work in the private sector for a while, possibly in advertising.

Have your qualifications been useful in your job?

I feel my construction degree has stood me in good stead with regards to graphic design as it got my creative juices flowing through draughtsmanship, civil design and architecture. I have learnt a lot about graphic design whilst working for Northcott from my colleagues and I feel that my diploma in graphic design helped me develop an all-round knowledge of design.

What sort of people are best suited to working in the NFP sector?

People who have experienced life and are generally happy to help would suit this industry. Diplomacy and integrity are also great attributes.

in brief

Graphic designer

$$$	34–45K
quals	BSc (Hons), Dip. Graphic Design
hrs/wk	38
life–work	balanced
flexibility	can walk away when it's no longer fun!

my day

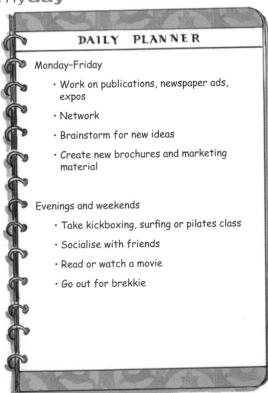

DAILY PLANNER

Monday–Friday

- Work on publications, newspaper ads, expos
- Network
- Brainstorm for new ideas
- Create new brochures and marketing material

Evenings and weekends

- Take kickboxing, surfing or pilates class
- Socialise with friends
- Read or watch a movie
- Go out for brekkie

find out more

www.northcott.com.au

CV maths tutor >>
consultant >> small
business owner >>
president

Daniel Almagor – President, Engineers Without Borders

When it's your business and your baby, time is a precious commodity, says 29-year-old Daniel. He established Engineers Without Borders (EWB) three years ago with the aim of improving standards of living in developing countries through the implementation of sustainable engineering projects. However, he is a firm believer in striking a balance between pursuing his passion at work and his passion for life.

In spite of this Daniel also runs Medivax, a national flu vaccination company, and gives lectures and presentations all over Australia. Since 2003 he has traversed many countries, including Indonesia, Cambodia, India and Nepal sourcing engineering projects, and was named as one of the 100 most influential engineers in Australia in 2005.

q&a

What motivated you to work in the NFP sector?

I've been volunteering all my life, usually at least a day a week. So the NFP sector was quite familiar to me. This particular part of it – engineering in international development – is something I've always been very passionate and opinionated about. I looked into it while I was at uni but found it very difficult to get involved in, so I started up EWB to make it easier for others like me to get involved in the future.

What does your current role involve?

A bit of everything – lots of meetings, staff management, strategy development, PR, fundraising.

Is there a workplace culture specific to NFP organisations?

As an NFP we are not driven by money but by values, which makes it a place of passion. We are interested in new ideas and seek input from everyone working at the office. Great workplace discussions and an incredible motivation to achieve our goals is the best way to describe the atmosphere at EWB, and in many NFPs.

We all work in an open office, so we work very closely together. There is also the feeling of an open-door policy – if you've got ideas, bring them up. This makes the workplace culture very informal; it's a very open and honest environment. I think this is indicative of the working environment of a small NGO.

What do you like most about your job?

Everything. I love meeting people, so the best thing is the contact I have with really wonderful people; people who are passionate about what they do, people who are successful in their work. It's great fun.

What do you like least?

I don't like dealing with the details. For example, having to write the text for a brochure – reading it through over and over and having to think of exactly the right words. It's hell. I am more a big picture man.

What interesting project have you been involved in?

I did a really interesting project in Thailand working on water filtration. It was fun to be a part of the village life there. It was also a very tangible project; sometimes we have to do a lot of research and planning, whereas this time we just put in a water filter and bingo – the water goes in muddy and comes out clean! So there's a sense of achievement because you can really see the results. There's something special about that.

Daniel doing 'field work' in Bali

Where do you see the growth opportunities in this industry?

In development as a whole there is massive potential for growth. There have been so many campaigns like Make Poverty History and Live 8 that draw international attention to the issues, so consequently governments are investing more money into aid, companies are taking on more tenders, NFPs' budgets are growing because more people are donating ... it's almost like a snowball effect.

What do you wish someone had told you about this industry?

There's one big thing I learned the hard way: that working with volunteers is difficult. When you're on your hands and knees begging volunteers to do things – that's no way to run a business. What we have learnt is to treat our volunteers as regular staff members – we have performance reviews and they can get fired just like everybody else.

How does your job allow you to achieve a suitable life–work balance?

Like in any industry, it's not the job, it's the person. Everyone has the responsibility to create that balance for themselves and has the choice to work in an organisation that allows and encourages it. We could work here 24 hours a day – there is always work to be done – but as an employer I tell my team I want them out of here at a reasonable time. If it's 6.30 and there are still people in the office, I kick them out. I am committed to that life–work balance.

How flexible are your work arrangements?

People don't get paid very much in this industry, so I try to give them incentives by offering them a more comfortable workplace. If someone wants to come in late and stay late one day they can. If someone needs to miss a day, they can make that up another time. We are very flexible. Everything is negotiable.

For example, Australia Day was on a Thursday this year and everyone wanted to take the Friday off. So I said, 'If we all promise to be extra productive the following week, and commit to doing the work that we would have otherwise done, then we can all go have a long weekend'.

MYTH
people in the NFP sector are there because they can't do anything else

fact
There are people in NFPs who would have made millions if they'd have worked in the corporate sector.

Where do you see yourself in a few years' time?

I would love to do a Master's in International Development, here or overseas. I would love to build up EWB to be as influential as something like Oxfam, say in 10 years time or so. I want to be one of those really influential players with the ability to make the world a better place.

How necessary are your qualifications for this job?

I feel like it's pretty crucial for the head of an engineering organisation to have an engineering degree, but it could be argued that I don't actually use anything of the degree itself! It's helped in terms of problem-solving skills and being methodical, but I can't put it down to any particular subject or exam that I learnt how to do that. Education isn't always about the specific skill set it gives you but the broader skills you acquire along the way. It's just about being conscious of learning.

Daniel (centre) with colleagues Blake Harvey an Steven Randell at EWB's 2005 National Conference

What are your tips for preparing an outstanding job application?

Know what you are looking for in a job, and think about what your interviewer is looking for in an employee. If you are applying to an NFP group, they want to see passion and professionalism. If it's a small business, they want to see that you are versatile and can adapt to different roles.

In all my interviews I ask, 'This is your area of expertise, but what would you say if I told you to draw up the budget? How quickly could you learn?' Small business for me means the ability to understand how the organisation functions from a wider perspective.

ⁱⁿ brief

President, Engineers
Without Borders

$$$ 35K

quals B Aerospace
Engineering/
B Business
Admin, RMIT

hrs/wk 50

life–work there's nothing
more important

flexibility 10/10

find out more

www.ewb.org.au

What personal attributes best suit your job?

Being a people person. It's all about relationships and your ability to communicate ideas to people.

What would you tell young people wanting to work in the NFP sector?

I would say it's the best place to work! If you're seriously considering it, you should read a book called *Affluenza* – it will help you justify to both yourself and your friends why you made a lifestyle rather than a financial decision about your work.

my**day**

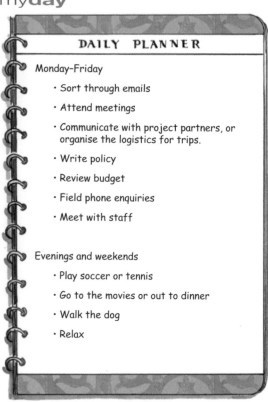

DAILY PLANNER

Monday–Friday

- Sort through emails
- Attend meetings
- Communicate with project partners, or organise the logistics for trips.
- Write policy
- Review budget
- Field phone enquiries
- Meet with staff

Evenings and weekends

- Play soccer or tennis
- Go to the movies or out to dinner
- Walk the dog
- Relax

Melissa Edgley – Project manager, AYAD program

Melissa began work with the Australian Youth Ambassadors for Development (AYAD) program in 2000 as a volunteer. Six years down the track, she is coordinating other volunteers as project manager, bringing aid to developing countries in the Asia-Pacific region.

CV international media
affairs coordinator >>
project coordinator, AYAD
>> project manager, AYAD

What do you do in your job?

The AYAD program is a government initiative funded by the Australian Agency for International Development (AusAID). In a nutshell, we send young, skilled Australians (aged 18–30) on short-term assignments of three to 12 months in developing countries throughout the region. My role is to coordinate the selection, preparation, mobilisation and support of up to 400 youth ambassadors per year.

In particular I manage the program's subcontractors, including in-country managers and pre-departure trainers, and provide support to AYAs before, during and after their assignment. I am also involved in monitoring and evaluating the AYAs' success in achieving their assignment outcomes – this means regular in-country visits and lots of report assessments!

What led you to this position?

My experience as an AYA in Vietnam brought me here. Austraining likes to integrate returned AYAs (RAYAs) into the management team if they can – this ensures that the team understands and empathises with the challenges faced by volunteers.

My interest in the development industry has only continued to grow and I've since completed a Master of International and Community Development through Deakin University in Victoria. This has resulted in a strong understanding of the theoretical components of development and greatly enhanced my project management skills. I believe all these experiences have given me the capacity to perform my current position.

How many people do you work with?

My team is relatively small – in total there are 10 full-time employees. In addition, we contract some 18 in-country managers in each of the countries we place AYAs, and also receive support from a number of short-term consultants.

fyi

Austraining is a government-owned Australian agency that specialises in human resource development and international project work.

What do you like most about your work?

The thing I like most about working in the AYAD program is the passion and commitment of all stakeholders – we all have some altruistic motivation to provide support to the developing world through capacity building and skills transfer.

Aside from that, I love the constant challenge of working with people, particularly in developing countries – nothing is predictable. I meet some truly amazing and inspiring people and never have a dull moment.

What do you like least?

I genuinely enjoy my job so identifying something I dislike is very difficult. If I were really pushed to decide it would be my occasional over-commitment to the program and inability to leave work at work!

Is further training encouraged in your workplace?

Yes, definitely. I've undertaken additional training in project management, project design and evaluation, Microsoft Project software and GANTT charts – and am a certified internal quality auditor.

Life–work balance – how much of a challenge is it?

This can be challenging at times – when you're supporting up to 400 young Australians in some 20 countries, there's always scope for emergencies outside of work hours.

In addition, I'm required to undertake a significant amount of travel, both overseas and in Australia. This takes you away from home for up to four weeks at a time. I try to maintain a balance by taking opportunities to explore the places I visit and making the most of my breaks from work.

MYTH

development workers can save the world

fact

If you can make a difference to just one person you've achieved a lot!

Where do you see yourself going from here?

I hope to continue working in the development industry – ideally returning to the field to be able to work with people at a grass-roots level. I'm particularly interested in community development in the Asia-Pacific region, working with vulnerable and marginalised groups to empower them and create opportunities.

What advice would you give people wanting to get into your line of work?

The development industry can be challenging to break into – you need a genuine commitment to the objectives, a willingness to study and expand your horizons and often need to undertake volunteer placements. You should try to find out more about the requirements for your particular field of interest, and speak to people who are already in the industry. Networking is also crucial as many opportunities are not widely promoted.

find out **more**

www.ayad.com.au

What are the job prospects like? Is the aid industry growing?

This is an interesting question as the ultimate aim of a development worker is to realise a world in which all people live free of poverty, discrimination and disadvantage – that is, we want to do ourselves out of a job!

Having said that, there's been growing recognition that people in developed countries can make a positive contribution to the lives of people less fortunate, and an increasing desire to engender security and stability through engagement – this means that aid work is growing. I hope that this trend will continue and many more people will have the opportunity (and desire) to work in an industry as challenging and rewarding as this!

in **brief**

Project manager

$$$	90–90K
quals	B Bus/BA, Swinburne; MICD, Deakin
hrs/wk	40–50
life–work	challenging but rewarding
flexibility	8/10

Ernestine Thompson – Nutrition manager, Heart Foundation

The passing away of her grandfather was one of the reasons for Ernestine's interest in working with an organisation like the Heart Foundation. Now 32, she's been in her current role with the Victorian division for three years.

The Heart Foundation of Australia and its various state offices was formed in 1959 by a group of cardiac physicians who aimed to improve the cardiac health of Australians. Since then it has provided more than $130 million in support of cardiac research, funded entirely by public donations and bequests.

What do you do in your current job?

My job is about making it easier for Australians of any age to choose healthier foods every day. We try to do this through education and communication but, more importantly, via structural changes like modifying the laws and regulations that influence what we eat.

What motivated you to work for an NFP?

I've always been interested in NGOs and charities. I read a lot about the Heart Foundation while I was studying – they're such a credible, well-respected organisation, and one of the largest NFPs in the health arena. Everything they do is scientifically sound, so I was really eager to work for them.

What's your working environment like?

I think we have a very friendly work environment. I've got a fantastic, dynamic team of motivated people. There are three of us who work directly in nutrition, and we're part of a larger team that works on other aspects of cardiovascular health, like exercise and psychosocial issues. There are 10 of us in total. We also work closely with members of the fundraising team and with Heart Foundation staff from interstate divisions.

What do you like most about your job?

I feel privileged to work for an organisation like the Heart Foundation. I'm very proud of what the organisation achieves, and I love the people – everyone is here for the right reason.

What do you like least?

Dealing with internal processes, which are a necessary part of the job but can be very time consuming.

What's the most interesting project you've been involved in?

One of my earliest projects was related to childcare outside of school hours. My role was to assist carers in the fields of healthy eating and physical activity for the kids in their care. They were so enthusiastic about our ideas that we managed to get government funding for a project called Eat Smart, Play Smart – A Manual for Out of School Hours Care. It's been a very rewarding project and a lot of fun.

Campaigning during Heart Week, 2006, L2R: Ernestine Thompson, Nutrition manager; Robert Flower, Melbourne Football Club legend; and Robyn Charlwood, CEO Heart Foundation (Victoria Division)

What sort of growth opportunities do you envisage for the nutrition industry?

I think nutrition is a growth area overall. More and more people are interested in the impacts of what they eat. At a policy level, governments and other key stakeholders are also increasingly aware of the long-term consequences and costs of poor nutrition. About two thirds of Australians are now considered overweight or obese, so dietitians have a vital role to play in the future.

What do you wish you knew before you started on this career path?

That it's quite challenging trying to change the world – and not everyone will agree on the best way to change it!

Have you noticed any difference in organisational culture between the private sector and the NFP?

I went from a very large public hospital to a relatively small charity – we have about 40 staff here – so the size of the organisation was a big change. Suddenly the CEO was walking past my desk and having a chat about my project or what happened on the weekend. That just doesn't happen when you work in a big public hospital.

I was also suddenly very aware of where the funding for my projects was coming from – the Heart Foundation relies on public donations and funding from various trusts.

How does your job allow you to achieve the life–work balance that suits you?

Working in nutrition means you're constantly reminded about the importance of a healthy lifestyle. There's be so much attention given to the idea of life–work balance recently that I really try to get that balance. But I'm not sure I've got it right yet. By not taking work home, living by the principles that I try to instil in others – such as healthy eating and physical activity – and enjoying my spare time, I think I do well most of the time.

Do you get financial benefits such tax-free status and the like?

Working for a charity, I'm able to **salary package** because of the organisation's fringe benefit tax. This means $30 000 of my income is tax-free, so effectively I get more take-home salary each month. I package quite a few of my regular expenses to take advantage of this benefit.

What personal attributes do you think best suit your job?

You have to enjoy working towards long-term goals – sometimes very long term. Communication is key and you have to be good at managing relationships. You also have to be thrifty, very creative with your ideas, and able to do a lot with very limited resources.

How necessary are your university qualifications for your job?

I completed a Master's in Nutrition and Dietetics, which is quite a specialised qualification and enabled me to become an accredited practising dietitian. Without this I would not have met the selection criteria for my current role.

However, a lot of my day-to-day work uses skills I have gained through on-the-job experience and mentoring from senior staff.

Do you have any advice for how to prepare for an interview?

When it comes to interviews, preparation is essential. Read through the essential criteria – that's often reflective of the type of questions you'll be asked. Know about the organisation – but don't ever pretend to know more than you really do.

in brief

Nutrition manager	
quals	BA/BSc, Deakin; Master of Nutrition and Dietetics, MND
hrs/wk	40–45
life–work	work shouldn't overtake life

my day

DAILY PLANNER

Monday–Friday

- Attend meetings and teleconferences
- Provide evidence-based nutrition advice to internal staff/other health professionals/other organisations
- Liaise with designers, printers, researchers, PR experts
- Prepare reports/discussion papers/proposals
- Develop consumer literature
- Prepare and give presentations/lectures
- Prepare project plans for the nutrition team

Evenings and weekends

- Cook, shop for ingredients at markets/delis
- Go for run or walk
- Read – mainly fiction
- Catch up with family and friends
- Go hiking

find out more

www.heartfoundation.com.au

Nic Clyde – Actions unit manager, Greenpeace

When Nic, now 37, first answered an advertisement for a Greenpeace street canvasser, he had no idea he'd still be with the organisation 13 years later. After two and a half years managing the actions unit, he still feels privileged to get paid for doing what he loves: organising non-violent direct action.

Greenpeace is one of the world's best-known environmental organisations. It aims to raise public awareness about sustainable living and environmental protection in order to force businesses and governments to become more eco-friendly. The organisation stresses non-violent action as one of its core values and main strategy.

What motivated you to work in the NFP sector?

It was definitely something I always wanted to do, but it didn't quite seem like reality until I stumbled upon a Greenpeace job ad for fundraisers years ago.

What does your current job involve?

I manage the actions unit. The unit helps campaign teams develop direct action strategies for various issues including forests, oceans, climate change and nuclear disarmament. When a plan is developed, our job is to look after the logistics. We also have to train new staff in first aid, climbing and boat-driving skills, **OH&S** and so on.

We're also responsible for the physical security of all Greenpeace staff, here in Australia as well as in Papua New Guinea, the Solomon Islands and Fiji. That involves ongoing risk assessment, security training and crisis response.

What other benefits are there in this job?

We have a couple of perks. If you want to buy a pushbike, Greenpeace will loan you the money interest free. And I think there is a similar thing with laptops.

Who do you work with?

I work in a team of four, plus a lot of quality volunteers. Quite often we are working on different projects, but we pool resources.

glossary

OH&S means:
– occupational health and safety

Next month most of the unit will be working in PNG on the paradise forests push.

What's your work environment like?

I think the conditions are progressive – we have a very good enterprise agreement. It's kind of relaxed; you can wander around in a T-shirt and shorts if you want to. There's also an emphasis on diversity.

What do you like most about your job?

When we organise direct action and it goes well, it's a tremendous experience. I love activism – it's just a lot of fun! I'm in an unbelievably privileged position to be paid for what I love doing.

What do you like least?

Burnout can be an issue. A lot of people work too much; they don't know when to stop because it's an NGO, it's a cause. Also, we can be hypercritical of each other because everybody here is so passionate about what they do – there are a lot of strong egos that sometimes clash.

What interesting project have you been involved in?

We've got a forest rescue station in PNG that's part of the push to save biodiversity and old-growth forests in the region. It's basically a camp by Lake Murray and part of that campaign is organising an international team of people to work with the locals there. We've managed to get a walkabout sawmill funded by a partner NGO to help run a project that promotes eco-forestry. So now we have to train the locals in how to use the new equipment. We'll also set up an export market for a small quantity of eco timber and that way the community gets more money back than they would from a dodgy logging company.

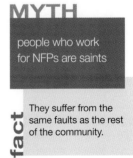

MYTH

people who work for NFPs are saints

fact

They suffer from the same faults as the rest of the community.

Where do you see opportunity for growth in this industry?

The climate issue, definitely – that's going to be the main battleground for the next decade in the global environmental movement.

How does your job allow you to achieve the life–work balance that suits you?

I would say the balance problem is something that a lot of people suffer from – working too much and not balancing their private lives very well.

How flexible are your work arrangements?

We've got time off in lieu provisions. So if you work a crazy amount of time, you can get it back at a later date. And we've got flexi hours as well. So yes, the job does allow you flexibility – it's just that a lot of people don't take advantage of it.

What skills have you developed on the job?

I just completed a week-long wilderness medicine first aid course because we need solid first aid skills up at the camp in PNG. I spent a month on the Arctic Sunrise icebreaker, learning the ropes of on-board ship coordination. I also did a fast rescue boat-driving course in Scotland, as well as climb training and scuba diving. And a lot of non-violence training – we are always trying to hone our skills there.

find out
more

www.greenpeace.org.au

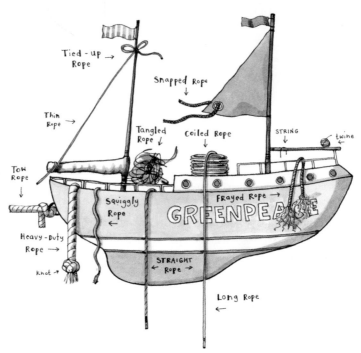

Learning the ropes of on-board ship coordination.

What ambitions do you have for yourself and the company?

I would really love to see a very strong, dynamic climate campaign take hold in this country. We have some plans for mass networking in place that will help transform our climate campaign into a major national initiative. I would also like to keep developing my own skills. So I'm looking forward to going up to PNG soon and expanding my logistical skills and my appreciation of different cultures. It would be great to work in some of the other Greenpeace offices around the world at some point too.

What personal attributes are important in this line of work?

Stamina – mental, emotional and physical. You've got to be committed to the cause and stick to your guns. You've got to be willing to take risks now and then. Also, it's important to be flexible. This is a very team-orientated working environment, so you've got to have good interpersonal skills and be able to work with other people.

What would you say to young people thinking about this career path?

The problems we're dealing with are not going to go away, so we constantly need more people working on these issues. We need to bring new talent into the movement and we need skilled, committed, passionate people who are up for it. I say, just go for it! A good way to get in is to volunteer, and be persistent.

in brief

Actions unit manager

$$$	63K
quals	BA, ANU
hrs/wk	40–50
life–work	It's going to have to improve!
flexibility	8.5/10

Catherine Wood – Campaign coordinator, Amnesty International Australia

Catherine, 37, used to work in a city law firm but made the switch to the NFP sector in 2001 and has not looked back. She initially started as a volunteer refugee caseworker and then worked under a number of contracts. She has been in her current position since 2004.

Amnesty International is a global organisation operating to defend the dignity and human rights of all people. The organisation undertakes campaigns, mobilises protesters and other supporters, raises funds and conducts research. It envisages a world in which everyone enjoys the right to personal dignity and freedom from abuse.

What do you do in your current job?

I monitor and analyse the actions of various governments in the 'war on terror' and their impact on human rights and humanitarian law. This includes analysing Australia's anti-terror legislation as well. I also coordinate Amnesty's human rights and security campaign, draft media releases and speak at public events on the issues central to the campaign.

What was your job before this one?

I was a commercial litigation lawyer, a role that was vastly different from my current role. Although the Amnesty campaign has a strong legal component to it, the day-to-day work is not legal per se.

What motivated you to choose the NFP sector?

I have always been attracted to social justice issues, and having gained some fantastic skills as a lawyer, I wanted to use them to help people less fortunate than myself. I believe very firmly in the promotion and protection of human rights, and I think the issues of human rights in the 'war on terror' are gaining more importance and relevance the longer it goes on.

What attracted you to Amnesty International Australia in particular?

I was attracted to AIA because of its independence from the government as well as from religious and political affiliations. It does

fantastic research and makes really relevant reports on countries'
human rights records – and it has a great reputation worldwide. I have
enormous respect for the organisation and the work it does.

Amnesty campaigners hit the streets

Do you work with lots of other people?

I work both in a team and across teams. I work closely with the
community campaigners who coordinate the teams of activists in each
region, and also with the communications team. Together we help
draft media releases, do interviews and assist in putting content onto
the AIA website. Since we're a national organisation, not all of my
team is in the same office as I am – my two supervisors both work in
Melbourne, so we have quite a few meetings by telephone!

What do you like most about your job?

Working on issues I am passionate about and for an organisation I
believe in. It's a deeply rewarding profession – working on issues
you care about, helping those less fortunate and giving a voice to the
voiceless.

What do you like least?

Hard to say – I don't think I could think of something I really dislike.

What interesting project have you been involved in?

I attended a conference in London hosted by Amnesty International
and another organisation, Reprieve, which brought together former
Guantánamo Bay detainees and the families of current detainees.
They gave testimonies of their experiences – including torture and ill-
treatment – and other international experts spoke about legal issues,

torture and the approach of the UN to the 'war on terror'. They also talked about what's known as 'extraordinary renditions', or the illegal transfer of prisoners by one country to another where they may be tortured or abused.

It was a fantastic conference and I was struck by the courage of the former detainees in talking about what had happened to them. I also had the opportunity to meet some really amazing people – from lawyers working on these cases in the US courts to other Amnesty International staff.

What do you wish someone had told you before you started on this career path?

The amount of public speaking involved!

How does your job allow you to achieve the life–work balance that suits you?

Human rights don't switch on and off at nine and five, so I'm often very busy both during work and after work hours. But AIA has a 'time off in lieu' scheme, which means that when I work overtime, I get those hours credited towards time off – it's fantastic!

What are your ambitions?

I'd like to be an international human rights lawyer before returning to work for a non-government organisation. Ultimately I'd like to see human rights enjoyed by every person in the world.

How beneficial are your qualifications for this job?

Having a legal degree is certainly very useful, but I would say that the Master of International Law is probably more directly relevant to my work. The skills I acquired as a lawyer have stood me in good stead, and strong analytical, communication and organisational skills are very useful here. An understanding of the legal system – both international and domestic – is also very useful.

What personal attributes do you think best suit your job?

The ability to focus on the task at hand, perseverance, professionalism, adaptability and a positive attitude.

Any advice for anyone looking to join the NFP industry?

Never underestimate the value of volunteer work. Not only does it help to familiarise you with how these organisations operate, but you also acquire some great skills and meet people working in the industry.

in **brief**

Campaign coordinator

$$$	45–70K
quals	BA LLB, USyd; Master of International Law, UNSW
hrs/wk	45
life–work	AI respects a good balance
flexibility	7/10

my**day**

DAILY PLANNER

Monday–Friday

- Read reports and respond to emails
- Review campaign materials
- Draft media releases and fact sheets
- Brief senior staff and consult with other staff
- Talk to other NGOs working on same issues
- Prepare plans for campaign strategies

Weekends

- Attend monthly meetings of another NFP organisation
- Meet friends
- Relax at home

find out **more**

www.amnesty.org.au

CV KFC checkout chick
>> market researcher >>
migrant resource centre
volunteer >> trainee
accountant >> internal
audit manager, World Vision
Australia

Sarah Cass – Internal audit manager, World Vision Australia

Sarah, 36, has been working for World Vision Australia for seven years. In a nutshell, it's her job to make sure the money people give to the charity actually goes to those in need. In her role as an internal audit manager she's been all over the world: Guatemala, South Africa, Lebanon, Jordan, Sri Lanka, Burma, Cambodia, East Timor, Vietnam, the Philippines, Vanuatu and the United States. She's most passionate about the Middle East, having studied it at university, but as she's currently expecting her second child she's now mainly based at World Vision Australia's head office in Melbourne.

World Vision International was established by American missionary Bob Pierce in the 1950s after his experiences seeing how children in South Korean orphanages lived. The Australian branch was set up in 1966. Programs include supplying aid to help developing countries recover from disasters, and an extensive child sponsorship network.

q&a

What do you do in your job?

My role is pretty varied but I have two main functions. I conduct standard financial audits, which basically means ensuring that the correct people are being paid within the organisation. Then there's operational audits – that's the interesting stuff. If World Vision runs an emergency relief appeal to raise money for an earthquake in Iran, or for tsunami victims, it's my job to make sure the money gets used for what the marketing people say it's going to be used for. It's my favourite dinner party conversation: 'What do you do?' 'I'm the one that makes sure the money you give to charity is spent properly!'

Do you have a lot of responsibility?

Yes, it's my job to make sure the organisation is credible and transparent. There can be problems at times given the fact that auditors are often viewed as compliance police rather than as partners working to improve things. Management can feel intimidated by the fact that I report directly to the board and they have no way of watering down what I'm going to say.

What led you to this position?

Well, I've always been passionate about working in humanitarian aid, so I was actually working for the immigration department in Canberra when I attended some function – I think it was a cocktail party – and I approached a director of the Red Cross. I asked for her advice about how to get into the industry and she told me that organisations like the Red Cross really need good, qualified accountants with solid corporate experience. She advised me to go and get three or four years of experience with one of the big accounting firms and from there the doors would open for me. So I went and got my chartered accounting qualifications, then one of my friends noticed my dream job advertised in the paper – and within two weeks I had the job!

Have you done any volunteer work?

Well, the thing is, when I first decided I wanted to go into the humanitarian industry, I did do volunteer work at a migrant resource centre in Melbourne. For my current role, though, volunteer work was definitely not necessary – the emphasis was much more on getting some serious corporate experience.

What did you do at the migrant resource centre?

Anything and everything really – it was while I was at university and I was trying to get into the immigration department, so I was doing anything from helping solicitors draft letters to helping newly-settled refugees finding their way to post offices.

find out
more

www.worldvision.com.au

What do you like most about your current job?

I love the fact that I'm helping improve the living conditions of people who haven't had the same opportunities and education as me.

What do you like least?

There's nothing I dislike about the role or the working environment.

What motivated you to work in the NFP sector?

I feel like I've got an obligation to society to help those less fortunate than myself. You know, you grow up very aware of the fact that Australia's a fantastic place and questioning how you came to be born here rather than in the darkest poorest part of India where they've got nothing. So it's almost a bit of middle class guilt I guess.

Do you travel a lot?

Not so much right now as I've got a young son and I'm 30 weeks pregnant! But certainly up until last year, my job was 45 per cent international travel. It really keeps you passionate about the job, because it's in your face and you're constantly being confronted by what you see. It reminds you that the work you're doing is actually making a difference to people's lives.

So you can see the tangible results of your work?

Oh yes, absolutely. You see some really heart-wrenching things. I once visited a street children's drop-in centre in Burma and the kids wanted to show me around – one little boy led me to this shelter shed with only vinyl on the floor where some children were still lying on the floor asleep. I was so overcome by how basic it was that tears welled up in my eyes but I had to hide them because the children were just so proud of their centre. It makes you realise that if charities weren't providing these services, these kids would literally be sleeping in the gutter.

In other places there are now water and sanitation projects where there used to be none – where people used to have to walk miles to the well and the water was all dirty and grotty. But now they're pumping fresh water in their village, and you know it's because of the public funding that's gone into that particular project.

What's the most interesting project you've worked on?

One project that stands out in my mind was conducting an audit under armed guard in a Palestinian refugee camp. They were building a hospital there and the director, as well as eight senior surgeons, insisted on giving me a full tour of the hospital, even showing me a couple of women in labour – I think they were trying to demonstrate that they were using the AusAID donations properly. It was just absolutely fascinating to walk through those camps and see with your own eyes all the stuff that you studied at university.

Have you ever found yourself in a risky situation?

Well, I wouldn't be going to the Middle East now! In my experience I've always felt very secure – but there were times when I was cruising round in four-wheel drives with UN sirens flashing, Kamil tigers on one side and land mines on the other. At the time you don't ever feel that you're in any danger – it's only afterwards that you realise, Oh! That was actually quite a dangerous situation.

One of Sarah's roles is visiting families

What's the most rewarding part of the job?

As an internal auditor you're there to identify how things can be improved, so if people are actually taking your recommendations on board then the organisation is going to be more efficient and effective. Knowing that you're playing a role in improving things is the most rewarding thing.

Do you ever get demoralised or disillusioned with the work that you're doing?

Occasionally. I've been to so many places and seen all the good work that charities can do, so when countries descend into war or conflict it's just devastating to think of all the infrastructure that's been put in place just being completely annihilated. So you do feel that all the good work being done seems to get swamped sometimes.

What sort of life–work balance do you have?

At the moment I'd say I've got a very fair balance. In a standard week I work about 40 hours, but it varies according to the type of review I'm doing. If it's a project that I'm not that familiar with I might do some research on the weekend or pick up a couple of 12-hour days. But I've pulled back a bit because I have a young family now and am expecting another child.

When you're overseas, it's a different story. You're expected to work 18 hours a day, six days a week, because every day you're there you're paying for a hotel, food, travel and things like that, so you try and get as much done as possible while minimising expenses. So there's not much of a life–work balance when you're out in the field.

What sort of benefits do you get?

World Vision is classified as a public benevolent institution (PBI), so we're entitled to $30 000 in fringe benefits. Effectively that means that $15 450 of our income is tax-free. We don't get time off in lieu for overtime though.

Where do you see yourself in five years?

I'll probably go back into the corporate sector to brush up on my technical skills. The thing is that NFP organisations don't have a lot of money for training – they just live in hope that they can recruit people who are confident and technically up to date, so I see it as important to be conscious of maintaining my skills.

Sarah on location

What advice would you give someone looking to go into the NFP sector?

You need to have more than just a bleeding heart – make sure that you have some sort of tangible skill set that can be recognised as having real value for the organisation.

Do you have to be good at maths to be an auditor?

No, no. What's most important about internal audit is having very good communication and interpersonal skills, because it's all about getting people to work with you. You have to be able to solve problems without treading on people's toes. So it's not about maths, and debits and credits and all that – there's much more consulting involved than in your standard accountancy role.

What are the necessary qualifications for someone who wants to be an auditor?

They need to be a qualified accountant with experience in one of the top accounting firms – what they call the **Big Four**.

How competitive is the job market in this industry?

Well, I was interviewed back in 1999 for this position and at the time it had actually been vacant for about six months because there hadn't been any suitable candidates. I think that comes back to the fact that because the money is not ideal in this sector, there can be difficulties attracting people with the appropriate skills. The irony of it is that when you get into the job, you realise the rewards mean far more than money.

What sort of personal attributes are suited to NFP work?

An ethical constitution and a desire to strive towards excellence. Does that sound too wanky? You know, sometimes people think you've taken the NFP role as a sort of cushy, backwater type of thing. So you've really got to have the right attitude in terms of why you're there – it's not because you want a cruisy nine-to-five job. And you certainly need to be motivated more by job satisfaction than remuneration.

What's your life motto?

Make the most of the opportunities you have, and demonstrate gratitude for them by using your skills to help others.

fyi

The Big Four are the four largest global accountancy firms: Deloitte, KPMG, Ernst & Young and PricewaterhouseCoopers.

in **brief**

Internal audit manager

$$$ 60–80K

quals BA, B Commerce (Hons), Melbourne Uni, Grad Dip Applied Corporate Governance, Grad Dip Company Secretarial Practice, CA

hrs/wk 40 when not in the field

life–work fair

Dean King – Support services coordinator, Leukaemia Foundation

Having worked as a nurse for many years, Dean felt he was starting to drift away from real patient contact. Now 37, he's been in his current position for four years and says it has allowed him to get back to the more important face-to-face contact with cancer patients and their families.

The Leukaemia Foundation, established in Queensland in 1975, now has offices in every state in Australia. It is dedicated to the care and cure of patients and families living with leukaemia. In 2006 the foundation donated two million dollars to cancer research, while the World's Greatest Shave, a 2005 Leukaemia Foundation initiative, had 100 000 participant and raised nearly nine million dollars.

What does your current role involve?

I spend a lot of time counselling and educating patients and their families, assessing their accommodation and financial needs, and liaising with other health professionals to optimise patient care.

What's your work environment like?

The focus here is people-centric, with the intention of making people as comfortable as we can on their journey from diagnosis to death. So it's a very caring environment. The current team is very, very supportive, quite cohesive and can debrief well together. Unfortunately, we did have one new member who didn't quite click, which splintered the group for a short while. It's a tight little group, usually very effective but sometimes fragile given the situations we are confronted with. We're all very autonomous but we also work really well as a team.

How does working for the Leukaemia Foundation differ from being a clinical nurse?

As a nurse I was very involved in the chemical treatment side of things, such as administering chemotherapy. Now I'm more into patient education, counselling, running support groups, assessing accommodation and securing financial assistance for patients.

What motivated you to work in the NFP sector?

I wanted to get out of nursing. I was being pulled away from the face-to-face contact with patients and families, and this job has given that back to me. As for the NFP angle, I just ended up here – I didn't choose it necessarily because it was NFP. I chose it because of the type of job that it was.

How do the public and NFP sectors differ?

The move from the public sector into an NFP group was a huge shock. In the public sector there's a strict hierarchy that you have to answer to. On a ward shift you have drugs at eight, drugs at nine, meals at 12 – everything is very, very structured. I came from that to something completely unstructured and very flexible. So I'm not as rushed anymore and can spend lots of quality time with each patient as opposed to cramming it in.

What do you find most interesting in your job?

I'm fascinated by the psychological components of cancer: why some people cope really well while others don't.

Dean King at work with the Leukaemia Foundation

What do you like most about your job?

Spending time with these amazing people with great inner strength.

What do you like least?

That we have to suck up to hospitals or doctors to get permission to look after their patients. You think to yourself, 'Aren't we all supposed to be looking after the patients?' There have been times we've been faced with closed doors and made to feel very unwelcome.

What interesting project have you been involved in?

At the moment we're developing a book for patients who'll have bone marrow transplants. It's something that hasn't been done before so it's quite exciting. It will be a guide that walks you through what happens before, during and after the transplant, and what you can expect after you go home.

Where do you see the growth opportunities in this industry?

The next big booms will probably be in stem cell transplants and in new drugs that are alternatives to chemotherapy; they are actually like a synthetic antibiotic. Some of these drugs are out there now – they're a bit raw but in years to come there'll be an antibiotic that will see the cancer as a bug and kill it.

What do you wish someone had told you before you started on this career path?

That you need to develop a mechanism to protect yourself from getting too attached to patients. I have had to learn it myself; it was never brought to my attention. I didn't even think about it when I first got out of training. I didn't let the kids dying get to me – it was the parents' reaction that I found very difficult to respond to.

How does your job allow you to achieve a good life–work balance?

It's flexible and the team is very supportive. If I have had a bad day, I can take some time off to get myself together.

Where do you see yourself further down the track?

I'm really committed to helping children. If I don't stay in the cancer line – and sometimes I do feel the need to step out for a while – I'd pursue something along that line, like child safety or adoption.

How beneficial have your qualifications been?

I honestly think the counselling degree could have been condensed into one year instead of three. The first two years of it were useless. They gave you lots of information but it didn't actually click with me until I got to put it into practice in third year.

I believe the problem with our current health system is that the university-based nursing students aren't anywhere near prepared as those who go through a hospital-based training program. I did both, so I say that having seen both sides of it.

What's the most important thing young candidates should know about this job?

Besides genuinely caring about and empathising with patients, you also need the practical knowledge to help them. You have to be emotionally resilient and maintain your professional boundaries. And try to remember: at the end of the day it's still a job.

in brief

Support services coordination	
$$$	50K+
quals	BA Nursing, USQ; Master of Counselling, QUT
hrs/wk	38
life–work	work hard, play hard
flexibility	8/10

my**day**

DAILY PLANNER

Monday-Friday
- Data entry
- Run patient counselling groups
- Organise financial assistance
- Organise staff education
- Telephone counselling
- Network with other organisations

Evenings and weekends
- Got to the pub or movies
- Play sport

find out more

www.leukaemia.org.au

CV student newspaper
editor >> freelance graphic
designer (London) >>
freelance journalist >> web
producer >> national web
manager

Stephen Cannings – National web manager, The Wilderness Society

After working for a number of media organisations, Stephen decided that there must be a better way for him to help make a change in the world. Now in his early 40s, he sees his switch into the NFP sector as less of a career move than a deeply satisfying lifestyle change.

The Wilderness Society consists of a national office in Hobart, a national campaign centre in Canberra and numerous other campaign centres throughout Australia. It describes itself as a community-based environmental advocacy organisation that aims to protect Australia's wilderness and plan for the ongoing evolution of natural life.

 q&**a**

What do you do in your current job?

It's a mix of things, from fixing broken links to planning whole new content management systems. It also includes web design, content editing, liaising with campaigners, formatting emails and internal training.

How does this job differ from your previous one?

I used to work as a part-time web editor for Greenpeace Australia Pacific. There's quite a difference between casual and full time work. When you're full-time you have more meetings, more strategising and more frustration – whereas casuals are there as doers, not thinkers.

What motivated you to choose the NFP sector?

I'd worked in media corporations for a few years and wasn't completely satisfied with what I was doing. I felt that I wasn't helping to make a difference. You know the saying 'If you're not part of the solution, you're part of the problem'? Well, I decided to change things up a bit. I decided I needed to enjoy the work I was doing as well as have a life – because whether you like it or not, they are connected.

What appealed to you about this particular job?

I saw it as an opportunity to take control and express myself – and hopefully change for the better the web presence of the society. The first thing I learned is that nothing happens overnight.

What's your work environment like?

Our team is currently expanding from two full-timers to include another three half-timers. In a small team you do what you have skills in, so I design and edit, while my colleague is more of a programmer. Soon we'll have a writer and some more hardcore programmers.

In terms of seniority and management, we try and steer clear of a vertical hierarchy so that we can all have a sense of co-creation and ownership.

Is there a workplace culture specific to working in NFPs?

The basic difference from the corporate sector is that you don't work in an NGO unless you believe in its core values. The money is not good, but the satisfaction can be great, which transforms your whole life. This is not a careerist's move – it's what you do instead of climbing the ladder elsewhere.

What do you like most about your job?

The best part is my workmates. They are a motivated bunch and I really respect them – we work in an environment of unconditional good regard. We are not there for the bucks; we are motivated by other things.

What do you like least?

Web work is necessarily repetitive and painstaking. Time, technical and resource limitations mean you have to temper your expectations.

MYTH

the NFP sector is
full of hippies

fact

Although you certainly
won't find any rednecks,
most NFP employees are
compassionate people
who just want to make a
difference. That some of
them may have hairstyles
unsuitable for banking is
neither here nor there.

What's the most interesting project you've been involved in?

We've been sending out a quarterly magazine for years. I recently
designed and implemented the online version, which was really
satisfying – already the organisation has saved money on printing and
postage costs, and reached out to members in a new way.

What aspects of the NFP sector interest you in particular?

The way the noble will of a few has expanded over time into much
larger entities.

Where do you see opportunities for growth in this sector?

Talking about growth opportunities in environmental organisations is
a misnomer. The ultimate goal is to succeed in saving the environment
and not be needed any longer! Admittedly though, as long as the
exploitation of the environment for short-term profit continues, there
will be a need for counter-balancing activist groups.

Logging in the Central Highlands, Victoria

How does your job allow you to achieve the life–work balance that suits you?

I get to work from home occasionally, since my Mac is superior to
the cheap PCs in the office. And last week I went rock climbing with
colleagues from the office!

How flexible are your work arrangements?

NGOs are perhaps more humanistic than other organisations. We're all
able to sit down with our supervisors and figure out what works best
for everyone.

Where to from here?

While I'm still honing my skills and learning new ones, I don't think of the next job. I try not to worry about the future – the universe will provide for you so long as you stay positive.

Are your qualifications necessary in this job?

I sort of fell into web management after working as a graphic designer in London. I think it's helpful if you do lots of jobs in all different areas. In some of the places I've worked the manager had been there so long he hadn't learnt any new skills for years. I think people who've worked in four different places over six years have much more to contribute, especially in dynamic fields like the media.

What should young applicants keep in mind when being interviewed?

It helps if you're friendly. More than anything people want to work with someone they can easily get on with. Don't be afraid to show your true colours – it's a sign of confidence.

What attributes are vital for work in the NFP sector?

Altruism, a lack of greed, and a lack of need for power. And a progressive outlook on politics.

in
brief

National web manager

$$$	40–50K
quals	BA, Curtin; Cert. of Tech., AMTC; Grad. Cert. in Writing, UTS
hrs/wk	37.5
life–work	best so far

my**day**

DAILY PLANNER

Monday–Friday
- Update website content
- Edit stories
- Web maintenance and administration work
- Process and tweak images
- Create html emails for member mailouts
- Design special sites

Evenings and weekends
- Hang out with friends
- Go to the movies or clubbing
- Play tennis or go running

find out
more

www.wilderness.org.au

Julia Cabassi – HIV/AIDS and development consultant, Switzerland

As an HIV/AIDS consultant, Julia's job takes her all over the world, working with different international and national HIV/AIDS and development organisations. Julia's work involves assisting organisations to develop and implement HIV/AIDS strategies and programs and improving their ability to influence governments to do what is needed to respond to HIV in their countries. Julia lived in Sydney, but is now living in Geneva, Switzerland.

q&a

What is your job?

I am contracted by different types of organisations including international and national NGOs and UN agencies to help them get better at their HIV policy and programming. I work on short-term and long-term projects.

For example, I am working on a long-term project in India that's run by the Futures Group and funded by the Bill and Melinda Gates Foundation. There are many aspects to this work, but a central part is to train people to improve their advocacy skills – so they can best make the case to community leaders including the local governments to ensure that funds are directed to programs which will have a real impact on those most affected by HIV. For example, it's important to have specific programs for particular groups, such as sex workers, as opposed to general community education campaigns alone.

I am also working on short-term global policy projects, such as a policy statement for **UNAIDS** to help guide national governments in addressing the HIV-related needs of refugees. National governments often forget they are responsible for refugees who cross borders escaping persecution or conflict in other countries.

What do you do in the project in India?

In India, the government often deals with the HIV/AIDS epidemic by doing general community education. It can be challenging for governments to address the needs of the people most affected by HIV, especially when this involves sex work, drug use, and sex between men. India is not alone in this. Many countries are struggling with

these same challenges, but may have only started to tackle HIV in earnest in the last five years or so. In Australia, we have learned a lot after 25 years of experience with HIV/AIDS and this is recognised internationally. For example, Australia's experience in developing harm reduction programs for injecting drug users, or responding to the fact that Australia's epidemic is primarily among gay men is relevant to the Indian epidemic. There is a lot we have learned about responding to HIV that can contribute to ensuring the Indian response addresses those most affected by HIV.

My job is to look at the big picture to make sure we're doing the right things. The Indian organisation I am working with is trying to get people to understand the nature of the epidemic in India. I give the people who run the programs the skills to convince governments, bureaucrats, religious leaders and community leaders about why we need to act in a particular way, including why we need to address stigma and discrimination.

So I don't actually run the programs, but rather I am a technical adviser who helps train the people who run the programs. It's my job to pass on the skills so I'm able to leave at the end of the project knowing it is in excellent hands.

Do you spend much time researching and scoping the issues?

You certainly need to do a lot of talking, listening, watching and reading of the environment at the beginning to make a start. But you have to get started so you do what you can with the knowledge you have and you ask a lot of questions along the way. With the project in India, I've learnt a lot as I've gone along. It's a collaboration – it's not about me coming in as an expert and telling them what to do. It's me coming in with some expertise and listening and learning and working out what they need to be doing.

I've just started a project with the **ICRC**. They work in countries in conflict and their main job is to protect and assist people affected by war. They do a lot of work in prisons, and with people who are forced to leave their homes and communities as a result of conflict. The ICRC are neutral, and work with civilians, communities and soldiers on all sides of the conflict. One thing they do is work with prisoners and prison authorities to be sure that people's rights are protected and their basic needs are met. I am helping the ICRC to think about how they can address HIV in this prison work, particularly because in prisons HIV can spread rapidly, but with the right strategies you can reduce its spread.

glossary

ICRC means:

– International Committee of the Red Cross.

What's your career background?

It's been a long, winding process! I trained as a lawyer and went straight into working in community legal centres in Australia. I spent about 10 years in legal centres, because I wanted to represent people who otherwise couldn't afford to be represented. I also worked to educate communities to claim their rights.

Through that I became really interested in lobbying governments to change laws that impact disproportionately on the most vulnerable. So for example, when reforms of domestic violence laws were proposed which I did not think would meet the needs of women, I would meet with politicians to explain the reality of these women's lives, to say, 'That's not what happens in reality, this is what happens'. And I could draw on the experience of my clients and the case workers to convince decision makers, including members of Parliament, about what law reform would be the most effective.

That was very rewarding and it was through that work that I became more focused on policy, advocacy and law reform issues that change the way that law and policy impacts on vulnerable groups – such as people living with HIV/AIDs, indigenous people, or victims of sexual violence. It is about changing laws and policy to better address their needs in a way that individual litigation rarely can.

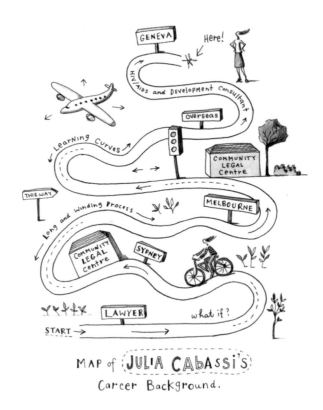

MAP of JULIA CABASSI'S
Career Background.

How did you come to specialise in HIV/AIDS?

I have always been interested in the area of HIV/AIDS. I was involved in setting up the first HIV/AIDS community legal centre in Melbourne. I worked on HIV/AIDS related projects with the NSW Anti-Discrimination Board, NSW Corrections Health Service, and other organisations. The last legal centre I worked at was the Inner City Legal Centre in Sydney which is on Oxford Street, and there I did a lot of litigation for people living with HIV/AIDS. Through that I started to do more policy and advocacy work around HIV and that built my experience that lead me ultimately to the work I currently do.

Do you need tertiary qualifications to do your role?

I've got an Honours degree in Law plus a Bachelor of Arts. I actually think I'm quite atypical because I don't have a Masters, which is usually a minimum requirement for more senior international work. My ability to work successfully internationally has been based on significant years of experience rather than on formal academic qualifications.

What is the best part of working for NFPs?

Working with such passionate and focused people is definitely one of the best parts of working for an NGO. At the ICRC, everyone has experience working in war zones. I think they are amazing – putting themselves at risk like this to make a difference to the lives of people affected by conflict. You always feel humbled by the commitment people make. It's more than work – it's a way of life, and they give up a lot to do that. That passion is something that makes NGOs exceptional.

What are the biggest challenges of working for NFPs?

Money is often an issue – that there are never enough resources to do what you want to do. Also, the NFP sector hasn't grasped well the need to invest in professional staff training and development. At NGOs or NFPs, due to such limited resources, there are fewer opportunities for people to train and take other development opportunities, which will help to ensure top quality management, proper supervision and thoughtful strategic planning.

How was your own development done?

By working in the non-government sector I've learnt as I've gone along. I've learnt from my peers and also to some extent from good managers – who are relatively thin on the ground, meaning I haven't been managed much. I've often been told, 'here's your new job, off you go, do it.' And that can be pretty hairy when there's nobody with more experience to guide you. I wish I had better access to such professional development and guidance as I've moved through rather than just learning by doing.

Are you working on all these projects at the same time? You must travel a lot.

Yes, it can be quite difficult juggling jobs. I move around a lot according to my clients' needs. I have lived in Geneva for the past three years. Next week I'm going to the international AIDS conference in Toronto where I'm the chief **rapporteur** for a one of the conference themes about building new leadership in the response to HIV. Then I come back here for a week and then go to India for two weeks. We're developing an advanced advocacy training manual and are field testing that manual with representatives from 30 NGOs based in the Manipur – in the north-east of India. When I return, I will continue work with the ICRC, and will likely travel to places where they are tackling HIV in the midst of or emerging from ongoing conflict such as northern Uganda and the Democratic Republic of Congo.

Julia and colleagues at the International AIDS conference, Toronto, August 2006

What is a common misconception about working for not-for-profits?

Some of the myths about the industry say that NFPs are not really effective and often disorganised. I just don't think that is true. While they are often constrained by insufficient resources and there is certainly a need for giving more training and development opportunities to the people that work there, there is another side to the story.

The strength of NFPs is that they represent, and bring the real, lived experience of the people that they work with and for. That is one of the most powerful ways to shape the response of governments and UN agencies. Without this deep insight and real expertise, many of the programs and policies would not address the real needs of the people who are most affected by HIV.

What's a typical salary in your job?

It varies a lot. Basically consultants work on daily rates. I set a standard daily rate – and depending on the ability of the organisation to pay and the extent to which I want to work with them, I can be flexible. If you were working in a full-time senior policy and advocacy position at an international NGO, you would probably be paid an equivalent of about $80K Australian – that's at a well-funded, well-established advocacy organisation.

What are your working hours like?

I get paid for between 160 and 170 working days a year. I work a lot more days than that to actually bill for those hours. Sometimes I work really intensely, basically for six months full-time and then I'll have a week off because I get back from travelling and I'm completely exhausted! This week I'm doing bits and pieces on all sorts of jobs. So this week I may work one day for one job, and two days for the other two. The nature of consulting is you just can't charge people for everything you do. There is so much ruminating time that goes in without pumping out a document or answering emails or writing a curriculum or running training.

Are you happy with your life–work balance in this job?

I know that it might sound like a shock to you but I think I've got it pretty right! My work takes up a lot of time in my life but it's very exciting!

And I do travel a lot in Europe and elsewhere. I go away just about every weekend to hike and snowboard – I do lots of things other than work. I have a really rich life here. I have a partner and friends. But I do miss my family and friends at home in Australia. I am happy with my decision to consult because the work is complicated and engaging. It is also tough, and I need the mental and physical space to do other things, and reflect so I can give my best to the work. There is nothing like a hike in the Alps to make you realise your privileges, and to make you feel inspired and optimistic about how important it is to try and make a difference to the global community.

What personal attributes are needed to work in NFPs?

You need good interpersonal skills, the ability to listen, learn and create a relationship with people. You need to be able to use your own expertise and also learn from other people and other cultural contexts. To be a consultant you need to be self-motivated, disciplined, and committed – you don't have a boss hanging over your shoulder telling you what to do! You need to understand how to be able to use your skills and experience to support others in developing their own skills, and to learn from them as well.

What's your life motto?

Purpose over personality. When things get tough with people for whatever reason, stay focused on your intention and motivation for doing the work.

Someone working in a full-time job works around 240 days a year.

HIV/AIDS and development consultant

$$$	differs from contract to contract
quals	LLB (Hons), BA
hrs/wk	varies
life–work	perfect for me
flexibility	I can work the hours I want

Peter Randell – Chief pilot and SA operations manager, Royal Flying Doctor Service of Australia (Central Operations)

Peter, 50, has been working for the RFDS for the last five-and-a-half years and in the NFP sector for 10. He is spending less time flying these days and more in the office doing administration and managerial work, but says he loves his job as much as ever.

Established in 1928, the Royal Flying Doctor Service of Australia is an NFP aeromedical organisation providing emergency and community health care to regional and remote Australia. The national office is located in Sydney and the organisation is funded both from government contributions and public donations.

q&a

What do you do in your current job?

I'm responsible for making sure all our flights comply with the regulations of the Civil Aviation Safety Authority. This means maintaining training and operational standards, hiring, firing and managing pilots, as well as keeping records. I also spend about 20 per cent of my time flying.

What motivated you to work in community services?

It's to do with a personal ethos of providing a service to other people. The fact that I like to fly aeroplanes meant I could combine the two. It wasn't necessarily something I wanted to do from day one, but the more I got into aviation, the more it became a goal.

What differences are there between NFP organisations and those in the private sector?

Smaller aviation operators are under great pressure to get the most out of their employees and that can develop a culture of its own. On the other hand, the major airlines are fairly well cashed up. We sit in the bottom half of the spectrum: we're not a big company but we're not a small company either. A Qantas pilot just does what he is told, whereas we are concerned with operating costs and making efficient use of our resources. We have all those people out there rattling tins for us to make money so we want to be good stewards of that money.

What's your workplace culture like?

Well, our overarching aim is to safely and efficiently deliver a service – that is to help patients. The actual culture on the ground varies according to the personalities working at each of the bases. Here in Adelaide a lot of our longer term pilots are getting towards retirement age. Another base is full of pilots who've worked for NFPs for ages and are used to living on the smell of an oily rag; their ethos is quite different again.

What do you like most about your job?

The variety is compelling, as is the spontaneity – as a pilot you don't know ahead of time what you'll be doing or where you'll be going. You'll get an hour's notice, or even less. But what I love is that we're in a position to put a smile on a patient's face.

What do you like least?

Shift work is the hardest thing to deal with.

What's the most interesting project you've been involved in?

I'm leading a project for the development of a fatigue risk management system, linked with the University of South Australia. We're researching fatigue levels and working out how to better manage fatigue risk. It's a three-year project; we're about half way through the first year. We hope to be a benchmark for emergency aviation organisations and to the broader community as well.

Where do you see the growth opportunities in your industry?

Our workload is highly dependent on Australia's health care system and infrastructure. When we see a decline in health services, as we do now, we experience a growth in our workload as a result.

MYTH working for the RFDS is as exciting as it looks on TV

fact Not every job is someone having a heart attack on Ayers Rock. The majority of the work is much more routine.

Peter takes to the skies

glossary

Get a guernsey means:

– be approved for selection.

in brief

Chief pilot and SA
operations manager

$$$	70–80K
quals	Air Transport Pilot Licence, Australia
hrs/wk	50–60
life–work	very difficult to strike a balance with lots of call-outs
flexibility	6/10

Where do you see yourself in five years' time?

Over the next five years I hope to be less reliant on full-time employment.

What qualifications do you need to be an aero-medical pilot?

You only need a commercial pilot's licence to **get a guernsey** with us – an Air Transport Pilot's Licence (ATPL) is preferred, but a Commercial Pilot's Licence (CPL) is adequate. You need a minimum of 2000 hours flying time under your belt, and 500 hours in command of a twin-engine airplane. Two hundred hours of night experience is also a prerequisite.

What personal attributes should young pilots cultivate?

Motivation, adaptability, decision-making ability, an affable nature, the ability to work in team environment and experience working in remote areas. Piloting skills are important to us but it's more important that the person is teachable.

myday

DAILY PLANNER

Monday–Friday

- Daily account of resources, outstanding tasks
- Review changes in legislation and aircraft systems
- Meet with superiors
- Manage day-to-day projects
- Monitor activity of pilots
- Approve leaves
- Hire/fire pilots

Evenings and weekends

- Work on private business projects

find out more

www.flyingdoctor.net

Peter Klinken – Director, Western Australian Institute for Medical Research

CV retail manager
>> high school teacher
>> postdoctoral fellow,
USA >> professor of
biochemistry >> director

Peter Klinken, now in his early 50s, worked in his father's duty-free shop while he was studying for his PhD in biochemistry. After working as a high school teacher and a postdoctoral stint in the US, he was involved in the founding of the Western Australian Medical Research Institute in Perth. That was in 1998, and the institute has now grown to employ 170 people.

Peter works from seven in the morning until seven at night, five days a week, at least one day on weekends and still finds the time to run his own lab with 12 researchers. He says that he is motivated by the fact that he loves his work, and wants to see the WAIMR become an internationally recognised institution.

q&a

What does your job involve?

I run the institute, manage funds and try to raise more money. I spend a lot of time lobbying politicians to secure funding, and I meet with other people who are interested in providing funds to the institute, such as our founding sponsor Wesfarmers. I also act as sort of a PR person, working with the media to make sure we get appropriate coverage for our discoveries, and dealing with important issues that are topical for society, such as genetics, stem cell research, those sorts of issues. In the meantime I still run my own lab.

What do you see as your most important function at the institute?

I set the culture for the institute. I try to make sure that I stress some core values to everyone who comes through my door.

The first is innovation: we are nothing if not innovative. Our business is the creation of new knowledge, so we've got to be really out there, thinking big.

Secondly, we have to have a sense of urgency. I don't want people sitting around feeling comfortable. I really want people to be moving forward – you have to be active, busy, moving on.

Finally, I believe we have to have a sense of responsibility, both to the community and the people who fund us. A lot for researchers just take the money and run. I don't want that kind of culture – I want us to really appreciate that someone's giving away their own money so that we can do our job.

What sort of work environment do you strive for?

I try to acknowledge that you can have very good people but it won't help unless you have a great environment to work in. You've got to have ideals – it's not going to be perfect all the time, but you've got to steer clear of the kind of nasty environment where people don't want to come to work. A happy workforce is a productive workforce.

In an organisation like mine you can come across some highly intelligent egos, so it's important not to go stomping into someone else's territory. Inevitably someone's going to get irritated somewhere down the line, so it's my job to smooth things over, or, better yet, avoid disputes in the first place.

What's the main purpose of the institute?

Basically all our work is to try and understand the genes that cause adult diseases such as cancer. There will never, ever be a pill that you can take to cure it – the reason we get cancer is because we've got an inherent defect in our machinery that replicates our DNA. And we can't get around that – it's just a facet of being human. But what we can do is learn to treat it better, and eventually ameliorate it.

In a nutshell, genes make proteins and the proteins do the work, so if you've got a bad gene that makes bad proteins, you're in trouble. It's often harder to fix the gene so we try to work out how we can get around that by focusing on fixing up the protein.

The analogy that I give is that it's a bit like a criminal organisation – you've got the bad dude at the top, but it's his henchmen who actually go out and do the crimes. If you want to fix the root of the problem, you've got to get the head honcho. Sometimes that's not possible though, in which case you have to deal with the symptoms and minimise the damage.

What project are you currently working on?

One of our main focuses is a gene called HLS5 – we've spent 10 years working on it so far. We're hoping that it may be able to slow the rate of some cancers. But the next five years is absolutely critical to whether it's going to turn out to be a hot breakthrough, or just another interesting observation.

Are you in a position where you can see tangible results?

No. Everything we do is in a laboratory. Every now and then we stumble across something exciting, and that gives us a thrill – but it's a long way from making a scientific discovery to finally translating it into something medically useful. So that's one of the things that I try to make a priority: making sure that all of our discoveries are translated into something that's good for the health of our community. It shouldn't be just mental gymnastics, but rather something that benefits mankind.

fyi

HLS5 is a tumour suppressor gene that may be able to be used to slow the growth rate of some types of cancer. Its discovery could lead to the development of a drug that could potentially even stop the growth of cancer cells.

What's the most rewarding part of your job?

Creating new knowledge. We're like explorers. We're going into places that no-one's gone before. We're seeing stuff no-one's seen before. And along the way we get to actually help people.

Is it difficult to secure funding?

Lately it's actually been remarkably good. It has been difficult in the past, but with the current economic boom the government is much more amenable to new initiatives, so it's really an exciting time for us.

Are your qualifications necessary in your current job?

They certainly were essential for me as a research scientist and an academic – but they probably don't provide me with the skills that I need now as an administrator and a manager. Basically I've gone into a role now that I didn't actually train for.

How competitive is this job market?

It's very competitive because there are more researchers than there are jobs. One of the big problems in Australia is that we keep training bright young scientists who are forced to leave the country because there are no jobs for them here. It's a disaster really – Australia can't afford to keep exporting its talent.

What sort of money does a medical researcher make?

It depends on the level of qualifications that you've got. If it's just a regular science degree, you can make up to $70 thousand a year. With a PhD, it all depends how far you want to go – if you're working in a lab as a postdoctoral fellow, you're looking at maybe $80 thousand. If you become a lab head or a senior academic, you might make up to $120 thousand. And then if you branch out and become the director of an institute or what have you – well, you get loads more.

What personal qualities are important for people going into this field?

They need to be passionate about wanting to create new knowledge and wanting to improve mankind. I want to see people who are prepared to ask big questions, are innovative and prepared to take on big challenges. They need to be bold.

Peter Klinken in the lab

What do you wish someone had told you about this industry before you went into it?

I was very naive when I came into it – I thought it was all for the good of mankind, but I soon discovered there's this thing called human nature. It makes for a very competitive environment.

I'll give you an example. When I went to the US for my first post-doctoral scholarship, I came up with an idea that was pretty wild but I thought it was worthy. I took it to one of my superiors to see what he thought, and he told me it was too far out of left field and that I should just forget it. But, three months later, he published a paper in a very prestigious journal with exactly my idea.

He ripped me off intellectually and gave me no credit for it, as though it was his idea. For me it was a rude awakening into the real world. But these things happen – you become a little more cautious, a little more protective, while still trying to retain your passion and enthusiasm.

Do you get to travel a lot?

A hell of a lot. I'm on a plane every second week. Last week I was in Melbourne and Canberra, the week before that in Tokyo and Hong Kong. I was in San Fransciso and Chicago earlier in the year. It's partly to raise profile for the institute but also on behalf of medical research in Australia, working for the state and the nation as such.

How do you maintain a life–work balance?

With great difficulty. It's a serious challenge because by the end of the week I'm knackered. I find that I just crash – I tend to veg out and have a sleep in the afternoon, go to bed early and then by Sunday morning I'm back at work again. So there's not an awful lot of free time for me personally, and not a lot of time to spend with my family. I've got three kids, but luckily they're pretty much grown up now – they don't need the old man hanging around anymore.

I wouldn't say that I'm stressed, though, because stress to me means that you can't handle the situation. I can handle it, but I just feel fatigued. I try to go to the gym two or three times a week and do a bit of physical exercise, but there are times when I'm so tired I just can't do it – and that frustrates me.

in
brief

Director, medical
research institute

$$$ 150K+

quals   BSc (Hons) UWA,
DipEd Scots
College, PhD in
Biochemistry

hrs/wk   60–70

life–work   not a lot of free time!

flexibility   can be arranged

my**day**

DAILY PLANNER

8.00 am	Plan for the day ahead
9.00 am	Meet with business partners, government officials or donors
10.00 am	Liaise with laboratory heads about upcoming projects
11.00 am	Meet with staff in my laboratory about research initiatives
12.30 pm	Prepare for upcoming events/ seminars I'm presenting at
2.00 pm	Assist staff with grant applications
3.30 pm	Liaise with business development manager, chief financial officer and PR consultant on current projects
5.00 pm	Attend stakeholder briefing session

find out
more

www.waimr.uwa.edu.au

Jonathan Treagust – Country program coordinator, World Vision Australia

Having grown up in Papua New Guinea, Jonathan was aware from an early age of the vulnerabilities that exist in parts of the developing world. After studying rural resource management and food security, he worked in a variety of countries before coming to Australia two years ago to take up the role of country program coordinator with World Vision in Melbourne.

His job takes him several times a year to the two countries that he coordinates the programs for – Thailand and Papua New Guinea (PNG). While his background has been in agriculture, Jonathan, 35, is now developing skills in other areas that World Vision focuses on, including human trafficking.

What sort of projects does World Vision do?

Broadly speaking, we work in three different areas – development, emergency relief and advocacy. I'm mainly concerned with the development area which can be broken up into two different types of work – special projects, which are usually just funded by governments and cover just one sector or area, and Area Development Programs, that are funded by individuals who sponsor children in a program in one country. Our Area Development Programs usually cover a broader range of sectors, so they include things like economic development, health, HIV/AIDS, water and education.

What does your job involve exactly?

I'm specifically looking after two countries – Thailand and Papua New Guinea, where we have national offices to coordinate all the work World Vision does in those countries.

I work in five different areas to support these National Offices and we do a lot of capacity building with the World Vision staff. We build their organisational capacity, we work together on the development thinking or the development approach, we also work on designing and implementing projects and on finding new opportunities, whether that's new projects or new funding opportunities.

In your job, do you get to travel much?

We travel perhaps four or five times a year, really depending on the level of need. Most of our visits go directly to the National Offices in the countries where we work and we do a lot of capacity building for their own staff. We also get the opportunity to engage with communities, listen to their stories and share their visions for the future.

How long on average would you spend overseas?

I would go away for between two and four weeks and I would probably visit eight different projects during that time.

Within a country such as Thailand, there's a central office, in Bangkok, and I spend some time there, on compliance issues such as accounting and reporting. More often than not, I am actually in the field in the various regional offices in more remote, poorer locations and it's there that I'd work directly with field staff – either setting up workshops, listening to their concerns, or maybe working on re-designing the project. From there we also go out for an afternoon or a couple of afternoons to communities and spend time listening to their specific needs.

What motivated you to work in the NFP sector?

I actually grew up in PNG as a kid, which I think had a lot to do with it. I lived in a rural location and traveled a great deal around there and the Asia region. I guess that made me more aware of the vulnerabilities that exist. But I think more than anything, what motivates me now is that World Vision is supported by relatively normal people, just like you and I. They're not necessarily the richest people in Australia, they're not necessarily the people who think they have all the solutions, they're just people who think they can make a difference, and I think that's a big part of what motivates me to make a difference.

How did you get into this kind of work?

I studied a Bachelors degree in rural-resources management and I used it to get into food-security and then agriculture development. I completed a Masters in international agricultural development and that's really the entrance point into the aid program.

So you pretty much wanted to be involved from an early age?

Yes and no! I was interested in the agriculture side and the rural resource side, but I wasn't sure where I would do that. I started out prastising that in the UK, America and Australia but then felt that my skills were better matched to working in tropical regions and regions that are more vulnerable than where we live.

glossary

Food-security means:

– a situation where people do not live in hunger or fear of starvation.

Are there many volunteers involved in World Vision and its project?

We rely almost totally on volunteers in the communities where we work overseas and I'd say that for every staff member that we pay, we probably have three or four volunteers who we don't.

Most volunteers come from the communities, they know the local languages, they are in touch with their own people and they are essential to our projects. But here in Australia, it's a little bit different to that.

In the department that I work in, we do have volunteers who come through, but not so many, and they'd be fairly specialist. We have interns or student volunteers helping us with specific projects for short periods of time. Right now, I have an intern who's helping us with a trafficking project in Thailand, for three or four months, and there will probably be the opportunity to go to Thailand at the end of that period.

So where do you find the interns?

We advertised with universities, or students come forward with skills they can offer. We don't necessarily need people with experience, but we do want people who are passionate about the subject and who are able to demonstrate that they are keen to learn. Other parts of World Vision, and especially fundraising, rely more heavily on volunteers, but for our team it remains difficult because of the complexity of portfolios and National Office relationships.

Have you got any advice for people on how to get started towards a career in an NFP?

It isn't easy but I think the first step is to really get out there and to look at international work and the most obvious place is to look at voluntary work overseas. There's a big difference between those who have volunteered for one or two years in a position in Vietnam as compared to those who have backpacked through the Northern part of India for six weeks. You get a whole different range of experience and different depths of experience if committed for longer periods of time. So the more experience that someone has overseas, the better. One of the best starting points is probably to look at volunteer organisations like **AVI**.

So is there much opportunity to develop your skills in your job?

I think it's good advice for anyone going into this sector to be a generalist, but to have one area of focus that you want to specialise in, to set you apart from everyone.

For me, that's traditionally been food security and agriculture but now I'm also looking at a lot more at areas like child protection and trafficking, because that's where my work is taking me. I'm really keen to explore that and do more personal development in that area to expand my skills set.

How much could someone in your position earn?

Probably half as much as they'd expect to earn. I think it really varies with experience and qualifications, such as having a Masters or a PhD, so there's a sliding scale I'd say between $45 and $65 000.

What sort of personal attribute suit people in your job?

Coming into an organisation knowing that we don't have all the answers to the all the problems is probably the best thing. Having an open mind and being able to listen. Being passionate about the solutions although not necessarily knowing the solutions yourself.

Are there any myths?

I'm sure there are myths that the money doesn't go to the field or that the majority of the money is swallowed up here in Australia. Yes, it does take money to manage large projects, money has to be spent on administration and on management. But we do regulate those areas very carefully and they're explained in balance sheets which are made public. At the end of the day, the majority of World Vision's money comes in from ordinary Australians and so we know we have to work very hard to be accountable for our spending and to make sure we transform vulnerable people's life in the most effective and sustainable way possible.

glossary

AVI means:

– Australian Volunteers International.
www.australianvolunteers.com

in brief

Country program coordinator

$$$	45–65K
quals	BA Rural Resource Management; Masters International Development
hrs/wk	easily 50
life–work	work pretty hard but flexible!
flexibility	very flexible

Ready, set, go for it!

What qualifications do I need?

The war on terror, trouble in East Timor, the Israeli-Palestinian conflict – world peace seems pretty far away sometimes!

It's not surprising that new courses on peacekeeping, conflict resolution and post-war reconstruction are popping up everywhere. Not to mention the ever-expanding range of environmental sustainability and health-care courses – there are now more options for study than ever if you're interested in getting into the not-for-profit (NFP) sector.

The good news is that when it comes to qualifications in the NFP sector, anything goes. Many charities are run just like any other big business, so they need all kinds of qualified staff – everyone from accountants to zoologists. Along with university and TAFE courses, there are increases in private institutes and colleges offering short courses that can add depth to a university degree or show potential employers where your special interest lies.

Many of the people we interviewed had some form of tertiary qualification. However, there are some people working in the sector who have developed their skills on the job, either as a volunteer or paid staff member.

Here are the qualifications held by the people who were interviewed for this book.

Job title	Qualifications
Actions unit manager	Bachelor of Arts (Political Science and Anthropology), Australian National University
Advocacy and projects funding officer	Bachelor of Arts (International Studies)/Bachelor of Business, University of Technology, Sydney
Assistant country director	Bachelor of Asian Studies (Honours), Australian National University
Australian youth ambassador	Bachelor of Commerce/Bachelor of Engineering, Sydney University
Campaign coordinator	Bachelor of Law, Sydney University; Master of International Law, University of New South Wales
Captain Starlight	Bachelor of Arts (Media), Macquarie University
Chief pilot	Air Transport Pilot Licence, USA
Communications officer	Bachelor of Arts (Journalism), Curtin University
Director, medical research institute	Bachelor of Science (Honours), University of Western Australia; Diploma of Education, Scots College; PhD in Biochemistry
Engineer	Bachelor of Aerospace Engineering; Bachelor of Business Admin, RMIT
Fundraising and marketing officer	Bachelor of Management Studies and German (Honours), Leeds University (UK)
Graphic designer/brand manager	Bachelor of Science (Building, Surveying and Construction) (Honours); Dip Graphic Design
HIV/AIDS and development consultant	LLB (Honours); BA
Internal audit manager	Bachelor of Arts/Bachelor of Commerce (Honours), Melbourne University; Graduate Diploma of Applied Corporate Governance; Grad Dip Company Secretarial Practice, CA
National web manager	Bachelor of Arts, Curtin University; Certificate of Technology, Advanced Manufacturing Technology Centre; Graduate Certificate in Writing, University of Technology Sydney
Nutrition manager	Bachelor of Arts (Journalism); Master of Science (Nutrition and Dietetics)
Project manager	Bachelor of Business/Bachelor of Arts, Swinburne University; Master of International and Community Development, Deakin University
Support services coordinator	Bachelor of Arts Nursing University of Southern Queensland; Master of Counselling, Queensland University of Technology
Youth support worker	Diploma of Youth Work, Campbelltown TAFE

Career FAQs qualifications snapshot, 2005–06

If you're interested in any of the careers you've read about so far, this is the section that will show you how and where you can get qualified.

University courses

If you already know what field your passion lies in – for example, engineering, marketing or nursing – you could do a straight Bachelor's degree then look for NFP organisations and opportunities overseas in which to apply your skills.

Alternatively, there are an increasing number of courses – particularly postgraduate degrees – that cater specifically for people interested in careers in third world development, aid, environmental and relief work.

Most of the relevant courses for people wanting to break into the NFP sector fall into one of these categories:

- health care and social services

- environmental management and protection

- advocacy, policy and development

- emergency aid and relief work.

To give you some idea of what exactly you will learn in these courses, there are some examples of undergraduate programs offered around Australia on the following pages.

Health sciences

Health science courses are available at dozens of universities in Australia in many guises – they can fall into the pubic health or international health categories, and elements of health science themes are always available through more specialised degrees such as nursing or Indigenous health. At some universities a Bachelor of Health Sciences can actually be taken in combination with a Bachelor of Nursing, Commerce or Education.

Bachelor courses in health usually span three years and can be pathways into specialist postgraduate study in areas such as health informatics, biostatistics or health promotion.

Bachelor of Health Sciences
Career prospects
Graduates work in nursing, disability care, health adminstration/management, health education/promotion, health informatics, life sciences, occupational health and safety.

Subjects covered	Skills acquired
Interpersonal skills in health care	Effective health organisation administration and management
Critical thinking in health care	
Legal/ethical aspects of health care	Transferable business and HR skills
Human bioscience	Ability to effectively communicate with non-health care professionals and the disabled/aged/mentally ill
Health care systems and delivery	
Health: a psychological perspective	Analytical skills for research and evaluation
Society and health: sociology and epidemiology	
	Research methodologies
Health research	

Example of a Bachelor of Health Sciences

detour

If you're keen on the health sciences, find out about related jobs in Career FAQs *Nursing, Medicine* and *Allied Health*.

www.careerfaqs.com.au

Most health science degrees allow students to choose specialist streams that introduce them to the various fields within the health industry. You might choose to focus on management, for example, where you will learn about the relationship between business and health care in order to run health organisations. Health education and promotion streams will be useful if you're interested in working for community health groups, self-help groups and the like, while disability studies can lead to work in community development, welfare and advocacy.

Environmental science

No major corporation these days want to get caught dumping toxic waste. Governments are petrified of the fallout from potential accidents at nuclear reactors. This is what makes environmental science such a rapidly expanding field, and it will only continue to grow as we become more conscious of our environment and the expertise needed to manage it properly.

There are more than 400 courses in environmental studies offered at universities throughout Australia qualifying graduates for work in environmental protection, state and local governments, land and heritage management, forestry, eco-tourism, mining, manufacturing and regulatory bodies such as the Environmental Protection Authority (EPA).

Bachelor of Environmental Science

Career prospects

Forester, eco-tourism manager, environmental protectionist, land and heritage manager, conservationist, geologist.

Subjects covered	Skills acquired
Sustainable resource management	Ability to communicate effectively
Biological chemistry	Data collection and information retrieval skills
Cell biology, genetics and evolution	
Aquatic zoology	Analytical and problem-solving skills
Environmental ethics	Policy assessment and management skills
Australian environmental policy	Research, evaluation and presentation skills
Toxic waste – risk and regulation	
Antarctic and oceans policy	Ability to work across disciplines
Sustainable tourism	
Freshwater ecology	
Fundamentals of soil science	
Insect diversity and function	
Earth's materials and interior	

Example of a Bachelor of Environmental Science

Environmental studies degrees usually span three years and most universities allow students to specialise in a particular area of interest, such as aquatic science. The interdisciplinary approach combines biology, chemistry, ecology and geography with environmental policy and management. Some universities will require knowledge such as high school maths, physics and chemistry.

International studies

With demand continually on the increase, international studies courses are springing up like wildfire at universities all over Australia. They teach the fundamentals of political and security studies, history, geography and commerce, with some universities lending particular weight to learning foreign languages and spending one or two semesters at overseas universities.

Others focus on studies of peace and conflict, with subject areas such as the philosophy and practice of non-violence, peacemaking and conflict resolution, and post-conflict justice and reconciliation.

Graduates find work in areas such as national and state governments, international and domestic consulting agencies, trade, education, recruitment, tourism, aviation, shipping, immigrant and refugee organisations, language centres, aid agencies, international regulatory and human rights organisations.

Bachelor of Arts in International Studies

Career prospects

Language specialist, political adviser/analyst, historian, manager or consultant in business, government or NGO, researcher, peacekeeper.

Subjects covered	Skills acquired
World history	Independent research methodologies
Globalisation and the third world	Ability to work in a cross-cultural context
International security	
International political economy	Language fluency
Development studies	Multi-disciplinary skills in HR, management and communications
Cross-cultural communication	
Migration and inter-ethnic relations	Ability to analyse policy and historical developments
International law and human rights	
Language studies	Ability to evaluate social, political, economic and cultural change
Current issues in international professional practice	
Comparative social change	

Example of a Bachelor of Arts in International Studies

International studies is usually taken as a three-year degree, often in combination with a second Bachelor such as business, communications or commerce. The major emphasis tends to be a one- or two-semester international exchange, where students live,

study and work in the country of their language specialty. Some universities encourage working internships, such as RMIT University, some of whose previous students worked with the UN in New York and London, and with World Vision in Bangladesh. Other universities organise placements at partner universities abroad, and will sometimes pay the airfare, insurance and student fees for you.

Students in a lecture about NGO, Engineers Without Borders.

Emergency management

Anyone who's ever watched the television series 24, in which the competent professionals rescue the American President from crisis after crisis, will be keen on learning about emergency management. You don't have to be a firefighter or ambulance driver to be suitable – more roles are opening up every day for crisis management professionals.

Bachelor of Social Science (Emergency Management)

Career prospects

Public sector: government, community and health care or police, fire, ambulance and state emergency services. Also private sector: insurance, mining or manufacturing industries.

Subjects covered	Skills acquired
Introductory sociology	Practical and theoretical skills for emergency management
Emergency management planning	
Foundations of psychology	Ability to effectively communicate with emergency, community and health services
Social research	
Emergency operations management	Ability to retrieve, analyse and evaluate information
Human resources management	
Business law and ethical theory	Transferable business management and HR skills
Organisational behaviour	
Community analysis	Basic sociology and psychology skills
Emergency recovery management	
Psychology of stress and trauma	

Example of a Bachelor of Social Science (Emergency Management)

Students of emergency management are trained in the fundamentals of psychology and sociology as well as emergency operations and human resources management.

Bachelor courses usually take three or four years. Graduates can find work in business and in government, as well as in NGOs specialising in emergency relief work and disaster management.

Degrees in emergency management usually span three or four years and use a multidisciplinary approach that combines practical and theoretical knowledge.

Key learning areas include emergency management, social sciences and human resource management. Most courses focus on prevention, preparedness, response and recovery, with subjects including psychotraumatology, emergency operations management, local government law and community analysis.

find out more

See Appendix for a state-by-state list of relevant university courses.

About HECS
www.goingtouni.gov.au

About Australian universities
www.thegoodguides.com.au

About admissions
www.uac.edu.au

TAFE courses

TAFE institutes across Australia are a great avenue for gaining qualifications if you can't stand the thought of spending years at uni, but you don't feel certain about jumping straight into a job.

There are heaps of TAFE campuses in every state and territory in the country that offer course specialisations you could use to get your foot in the door in NFP organisation.

TAFE courses are taught at different levels and sometimes you will need to have completed the basic certificates to move on to the more advanced diploma stage. For each course you will usually find Certificates I through IV, followed by a Diploma and Advanced Diploma.

Here are some examples of TAFE courses that you might find useful.

Aboriginal and Torres Strait Islander health

Health courses with a focus on Aboriginal and Torres Strait Islander issues are available at many TAFE campuses throughout Australia and are aimed at students of both Indigenous and non-Indigenous backgrounds.

Subject areas usually include a focus on cultural awareness and sensitivity, community needs and background of Aboriginal health issues in Australia.

Certificate I in Aboriginal and Torres Strait Islander Health	
Topics covered	Skills acquired
Introduction to health	Field experience in city and regional health
Homemakers' skills	
Healthy foods	Ability to make healthy lifestyle choices
Shopping wise	Ability to administer basic first aid
My community	Ability to effectively and sensitively communicate with patients of all backgrounds
Senior first aid	
Women's health	Competency in caring for patients of all ages
Care giving – babies, children, adolescent, disability, aged	

Example of a Certificate I in Aboriginal and Torres Strait Islander Health

Most courses of this kind involve a minimum of 360 hours of classroom time that can be done either on a part-time or full-time basis. There are no minimum entrance requirements but if the course is oversubscribed at a particular TAFE campus prospective students may require endorsement from an Aboriginal community or local agency to support their application. Graduates are qualified for work in Aboriginal child and community health care and remote area assistance.

Conservation and land management

If you've always wanted to work outdoors, you might as well do it for a good cause – a TAFE certificate in conservation and land management is a useful entry-level qualification for you. You'll be able to go into parks and wildlife restoration, pest management, heritage protection, forestry or any related field. Core study units usually include weed control, project work, construction and planting.

Certificate I in Aboriginal and Torres Strait Islander Health	
Topics covered	Skills acquired
Observe environmental work practices	Operating four-wheel drives vehicle in off-road conditions
Provide basic first aid	Using hazardous substances safely
Work effectively in the industry	Responding to wildfire
Participate in workplace communications	Planting trees and shrubs
Conservation and land management	Operating and maintaining chainsaws
	Treating plants, pests, diseases and disorders
Follow OH&S procedures	Applying animal trapping techniques
	Operating in isolated and remote situations
	Carrying out natural area restoration works

Example of a Certificate II in Conservation and Land Management

These courses can be done in conjunction with traineeships with particular companies, or on a part-time basis if you're already working full-time. Keep in mind that the selection and availability of elective units may vary between TAFE campuses.

Graduates are likely to find work in such areas as Indigenous land management, as field officers of the Parks and Wildlife Service or Green Corps, bush regenerators, rangers or environmental consultants.

Government, policy and development

TAFE courses in policy and development are not as numerous and widespread as, say, environmental or health studies. Most courses in this vein are likely to be found in the ACT at the Canberra Institute of Technology.

These courses can be used as bridging courses to move into university studies in policy and development or law, or as passports into the public service as an administrative or executive officer. If it's an NFP role that you're after, these courses can open doors for graduates to work in NGOs as development officers, international observers, supervisors and project managers.

Diploma of Government Policy Development
Core subjects
Promote the values and ethos of public service
Undertake research and analysis
Promote diversity
Use complex workplace communication strategies
Promote compliance with legislation in the public sector
Develop organisation policy
Advise on organisation policy
Develop public policy
Provide policy advice
Monitor and maintain workplace safety

Example of a Diploma of Government Policy Development

These courses tend to last between 15 and 20 weeks, with up to 20 hours per week of face-to-face classroom time. Graduates are qualified for work in the public sector, particularly in senior management roles. Applicants must have a Year 12 Certificate or equivalent and be currently working in the public sector.

Public safety and emergency management

Some TAFE courses in emergency management are specifically targeted at people already working in the emergency services, while others have a specific focus on supervision and management roles. You will learn the basic competencies required for fighting fires, responding to rescue calls, dealing with hazardous materials and managing emergency operations. Other study areas include learning how to operate firefighting equipment, maintain safety at accident sites, and navigate urban and rural environments.

find out more

TAFE websites

www.tafe.nsw.edu.au

www.tafe.vic.gov.au

www.tafe.qld.gov.au

www.tafe.tas.edu.au

www.tafe.sa.edu.au

www.tafe.wa.edu.au

www.centralian.nt.edu.au

www.cdu.edu.au

www.cit.act.edu.au

Advanced Diploma of Public Safety (Emergency Management)	
Core subjects	Skills acquired
Establish context and develop risk evaluation criteria	Control multi-agency emergency situations
	Manage public safety responsibilities
Identify, analyse and evaluate risk	Manage organisational communication strategies
	Promote a learning environment in the workplace
Determine treatment strategies	
	Manage marketing requirements
Manage treatment strategy implementation	Manage physical resources
	Develop public safety awareness programs
Manage human resources	
	Manage media requirements at a major incident
Manage financial resources	Establish occupational health and safety system
	Represent organisations in judicial settings

Example of an Advanced Diploma of Public Safety (Emergency Management)

You can take a course in emergency management at various TAFEs as well as through the Australian School of Emergency Management, which is based in regional Victoria and delivers courses both externally and online.

The main focus is on planning for major risks and the multi-organisational managing of emergencies, such as fires, floods and severe storms. These courses also involve looking at community and workplace safety.

Short courses

There are lots of private institutes, organisations and educational consultancies across Australia that hold short courses lasting from a day or two to several weeks. Many specialise in fields relevant to NFP and NGO work.

Below are some examples of the courses on offer at the main research institutes and private colleges in Australia.

Burnet Institute

One of the largest private institutes in Australia in the field of health is the Macfarlane Burnet Institute for Medical Research and Public Health. Located in Melbourne, the institute runs week-long courses each year on topics such as:

- public health in complex disaster settings

- primary health care in developing countries

- communicable disease control in developing countries

- field methods for international health planning and evaluation

- managing community-based HIV programs in developing countries

- nutritional issues in developing countries

- health of women and children in developing countries.

Much of the training available at the institute is offered in conjunction with the University of Melbourne, Monash University, RMIT University, LaTrobe University and University Udayana in Indonesia.

Djanbung Gardens Permaculture Education Centre

The **Permaculture** Education Centre in Nimbin is an active example of sustainability in action. With its subtropical and tropical permaculture systems on display, it is one of the largest training and demonstration sites for permaculture in Australia. The centre hosts a number of courses ranging from intensive two-month workshops to full-time, year-long courses. Some of those currently on offer are shown below.

- Ecovillage: sustainable community and human settlement design

- Bushfoods and restoration ecology

- Organic small crop production

- Diploma of Permaculture

- Overseas permaculture projects

- Sustainable aid and overseas development.

The centre also offers residential internships to full-time students who want to live on site.

glossary

Permaculture means:

– creating a sustainable habitat and lifestyle by integrating the principles of ecology, organic gardening, architecture and agroforestry in an ethical way.

Australian Council for International Development

Based in Canberra, the Australian Council for International Development is an independent association comprising some 80 NGOs across Australia. Its aim is to uphold human rights, dignity and standards of living. The council hosts a full calendar of conferences, seminars and intensive course dedicated to achieving sustainable human development worldwide. Courses conducted in 2006 give an overview of the types of courses on offer.

- Facilitation skills and participatory approaches for working in development projects
- Education and development in the Asia-Pacific region
- Issues in governance and development
- Measuring effectiveness in humanitarian and development aid
- Humanitarian logistics
- Capacity building in Indigenous communities
- Participatory project management

Council courses vary from one-off, one-day seminars to full-week programs.

Emergency Management Australia Institute

Located at Mount Macedon in Victoria, the Emergency Management Australia Institute runs a number of short courses, workshops and seminars each year that are funded in part by the government.

Some courses on offer are shown below.

- Advanced Diploma in Public Safety
- Graduate Certificate in Emergency Management
- Civil defence in the 21st century
- Health aspects of chemical, biological and radiological incidents
- Disaster medicine
- Recovery management program

Courses at the institute itself can last from two to four days, while others are conducted by tutors in various locations around Australia.

www.burnet.edu.au
www.permaculture.com.au
www.acfid.asn.au
www.ema.gov.au

Developing your skills by volunteering

If the idea of volunteering makes you think of picking mothballs from crochet cardigans behind the counter of a musty old op-shop, think again. Volunteering doesn't have to mean slave labour and no reward.

Not only is it a good way to gain the necessary experience you'll need to break into the NFP sector, it also allows you to 'try before you buy'. NFPs are very different to the corporate environment, so it is worthwhile checking out if the workplace culture suits you. And of course, volunteer work looks great on your résumé!

It is important to know that not all volunteer jobs lead directly to paid work. Most NFP organisations need to maintain a certain quota of volunteers – many receive funds based on maintaining these quotas. So not all volunteer roles have advancement opportunities. Nor do volunteer jobs necessarily lead to jobs within that organisation – however, they may lead to other jobs in the broader job market.

> I think volunteering is a great way for young people to actually experience the NFP sector and assess whether or not it's what they really want.
> While volunteering may not always be a linear path to a paid job, it really can add to their skill set and it's a way of exposing them to certain careers before they actually commit.
> Kylee Bates, Deputy director, Volunteering Australia

So, what can you really expect to gain from volunteering?

A lot more than stuffing envelopes all day, that's for sure. The escalating trend of young people volunteering has allowed many organisations to delegate projects that will provide them with real skills and experience – even if there is still a bit of envelope stuffing to be done.

When enquiring about a volunteering position, the key is to ask what kind of skills the job or project will give you. It's also important to state what your expectations are. This way you can be matched with a volunteering role in a way that benefits both you and the organisation equally.

You should also ask about training opportunities. Volunteering Australia encourages organisations to include their volunteers in the same in-house training they'd give their paid staff.

As a volunteer – in fact, in any position in any job – you should feel absolutely comfortable asking your manager for a performance review

Helpful volunteer websites

www.svm.net.au

www.nvsc.org.au

www.conservationvolunteers
.com.au/training.htm

www.skillspassport.com.au

www.govolunteer.com.au

www.volunteering.com.au

www.volunteeringsa.org.au

www.volunteeringqueensland
.org.au

www.volunteer.org.au

www.voltasinc.com

www.volunteeract.com.au

www.volunteeringvictoria
.com.au

www.australianvolunteers.com

so that you can get some feedback about how you're going and where you can make improvements. Taking constructive criticism on board is also an excellent way of building of your self-confidence both in your own abilities and in interacting with management.

Your rights as a volunteer

- Make sure you've been given a clear description of your position and duties. This is important so that you know what your employers will expect of you and what the parameters are so you don't put yourself or the organisation at risk.

- You have the right to be reimbursed for any out-of-pocket expenses incurred on behalf of the organisation. So if the manager asks you to drop by the newsagent and pick up some photocopy paper, you should be reimbursed for it. If you're asked to deliver something to another organisation, your transport costs should be covered.

- Check that you're insured while you are working with the organisation. Most good organisations make provisions to cover volunteers if they're injured in the workplace.

- There are also the usual expectations you would have as a paid worker, such as clear communication from your superiors and the right to receive training so you can do your job properly.

How do I get that job?

There are plenty of ways that you can find yourself working for a good cause. Like many jobs and industries, word of mouth is important so make use of any contacts that you have to get your name in front of the right people – those who make the decisions.

How are people recruited?

Most NFP organisations either have HR departments or personnel that are responsible for facilitating the employment of staff. Many of them will offer jobs internally before recruiting externally.

> There is a tendency to look to in-house recruitment before advertising externally. Within Mission Australia, we give internal employees the opportunity to apply for every position that arises. We advertise on the internal website for two weeks, and then have the option to advertise externally as well.
> Ken Tapfield, HR manager, Mission Australia

There are a number of ways in which NFPs recruit staff:

- by placing advertisements in the major newspapers, employment newspapers and on employment and specialist websites

- by using a recruitment agency or headhunting company for specialist and senior positions

- by using personal contacts and/or the NFP network.

To be a successful job seeker, you will need to cover all your bases – don't just focus on one.

Advertisements

Job advertisements appear in the newspapers such as the major dailies and online at job search sites such as seek.com.au.

Some organisations also advertise jobs on their website, which, for them, has the advantage of attracting people interested in the work that they do or already scoping out the organisation.

Recruitment agencies

While most recruitment is done by in-house staff, NFPs do at times use recruitment agencies, particularly when it comes to employing senior staff in management positions. According to Elizabeth Varley, Director of Challenge Consulting Australia, many recruitment agencies have now added NFPs to their business streams.

Recruitment companies work on behalf of employers to help them fill vacancies within their organisations. The recruiting agency will usually take responsibility for advertising the position, sifting through applications and conducting the first round of interviews.

They then provide their client – the employer – with a shortlist of people they think are qualified to do the job and are best suited to the organisation. The employer will then interview the selected candidates and usually make a selection from this group.

As a job applicant, you will never be charged a fee for using the services of a recruiter.

Networking

One of the buzzwords of the 90s, networking is arguably your most important tool as a jobseeker. Whether you're a volunteer, intern or CEO, building networks with people in the industry can mean the difference between getting the job you love or floundering in the wasteland of unsatisfied workers.

So how do you network? Does it really mean sneaking into fancy parties and schmoozing with the head honchos? Don't you have to have bucketloads of confidence – and a bit of a reckless streak – for that?

In fact, networking is much more simple and everyday than that. You're probably doing it already without even realising it! One of the basic stepping stones to building your network is simply keeping a record of the contact details of people you've worked with, and keeping in touch with them. You never know when someone will need

your skills, but they can't give you a job if they can't find you. Even an annual visit or email can keep your name current in someone's mind, and may lead to the job you've always wanted.

Once you've made it into the industry, join your professional organisation or union, and get active in the issues of interest to your colleagues. The effort you put in might improve your own conditions or situation, and help expand your own network as well.

What are recruiters looking for?

Let's talk to some people who can tell you what they are looking for when they recruit staff.

Lyn Goldsworthy, NFP Consultant

Lyn has worked in the NFP sector since 1982, with 19 of those years as a campaigner for Greenpeace International. She was also responsible for setting up Greenpeace offices in Thailand, the Philippines, Indonesia and India, as well as hiring and training the new staff. She now works as a training, management and advocacy consultant for NFP organisations.

What are you looking for when you employ people in an NFP organisation?

There are a few things. First of all, knowledge and experience with the issues associated with the job.

Next, passion and commitment to the NFP sector in general – they have to fit in with the NFP culture – as well as the particular objectives of the organisation.

All this needs to be combined with professionalism, efficiency and boundless optimism.

Do you think there are personal attributes that are better suited to working in an NFP organisation? If so, what are they?

Personal responsibility is important. You can't view an NFP job as something to be done just between nine and five, so it often requires a more flexible approach and greater commitment.

Passion isn't essential, but if one is not passionate about the organisation's objectives or sphere of interest, it can make it really hard to do the job and stay enthusiastic and committed.

Also, the capacity to say 'no' and maintain personal life is very important – you shouldn't become completely wedded to or overwhelmed by the job.

If people want to work for an NFP organisation, how do you suggest they break in?

First of all, identify the particular job you are interested in, and ensure your education is relevant to that. You should gain a experience in related jobs – do some volunteer work.

Be vigilant, patient and persistent!

Stand out from the crowd

Like the door-to-door salesman of old, you've got to be able to sell, sell, sell – except we're not talking about vacuum cleaners or encyclopedias, we're talking about selling you.

So treat your application as the sales pitch to get your foot in the door.

STAND OUT FROM THE CROWD

People have to realise that a CV is like a sales document. If you can get your foot in the door and get in front of the person, then it is up to you to make the sale.

Elizabeth Varley, Director, Challenge Consulting Australia

Let's look at what you can do to wow any potential employer.

Create an outstanding application

In case you think the application process is different in the NFP sector, think again.

> Formal application is the same as would be expected in the general community, with at least one formal interview. For senior jobs there are usually two interviews. This is all part of seeing the job as a real and professional job.
> Lyn Goldsworthy, NFP consultant

And like all industries, your application is the key to getting that all-important interview.

> A job application is usually the first opportunity that an applicant has of trying to influence a prospective employer. As in life, first impressions are important. A well-structured and well-written application that demonstrates the applicant's education, work history and skills will enhance the applicant's chance of securing a job interview.
> Sam Broughton, Fundraising manager, Salvation Army

We're now going look at how to do that with each element of a great application:

- preparing your résumé
- writing your cover letter
- addressing the selection criteria.

The résumé

Like a headline in a newspaper, your résumé should sell and tell, which means it should concisely and precisely tell the recruiter what skills and experience you have and why they make you perfect for the job.

If you are just starting out, your résumé should not be more than two pages. With more experience comes the need for greater length, so you can extend it to three pages.

What you have to remember is that less is always more, especially if employers or recruiters are wading through a number of applications.

> It should provide sufficient information to provide summary and insight into skills and experience of the candidate without requiring 30 minutes to read!
> Lyn Goldsworthy, NFP consultant

So what is in and what is out?

The basic elements of your résumé shouldn't really change. What changes for each application is the focus of the content.

The following is an example of a well-presented résumé.

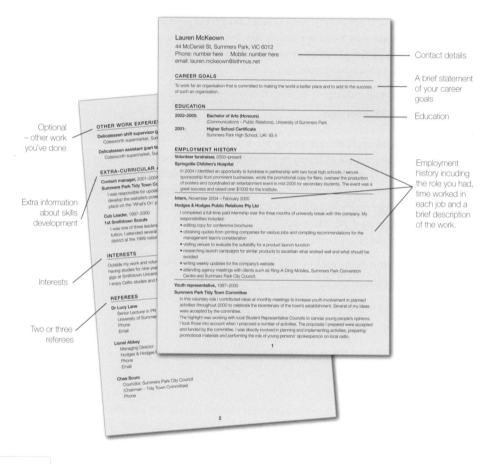

Optional – other work you've done

Extra information about skills development

Interests

Two or three referees

Contact details

A brief statement of your career goals

Education

Employment history including the role you had, time worked in each job and a brief description of the work.

Lauren McKeown
44 McDaniel St, Summers Park, VIC 6012
Phone: number here   Mobile: number here
email: lauren.mckeown@isthmus.net

CAREER GOALS

To work for an organisation that is committed to making the world a better place and to add to the success of such an organisation.

EDUCATION

2002–2005:   Bachelor of Arts (Honours)
              (Communications – Public Relations), University of Summers Park

2001:   Higher School Certificate
              Summers Park High School, UAI: 93.4

EMPLOYMENT HISTORY

Volunteer fundraiser, 2003–present
Springville Children's Hospital
In 2004 I identified an opportunity to fundraise in partnership with two local high schools. I secured sponsorship from prominent businesses, wrote the promotional copy for fliers, oversaw the production of posters and coordinated an entertainment event in mid 2005 for secondary students. The event was a great success and raised over $1000 for the Institute.

Intern, November 2004 – February 2005
Hodges & Hodges Public Relations Pty Ltd
I completed a full-time paid internship over the three months of university break with this company. My responsibilities included:
• editing copy for conference brochures
• obtaining quotes from printing companies for various jobs and compiling recommendations for the management team's consideration
• visiting venues to evaluate the suitability for a product launch function
• researching launch campaigns for similar products to ascertain what worked well and what should be avoided
• writing weekly updates for the company's website
• attending agency meetings with clients such as Ring-A-Ding Mobiles, Summers Park Convention Centre and Summers Park City Council.

Youth representative, 1997–2000
Summers Park Tidy Town Committee
In this voluntary role I contributed ideas at monthly meetings to increase youth involvement in planned activities throughout 2000 to celebrate the bicentenary of the town's establishment. Several of my ideas were accepted by the committee.
The highlight was working with local Student Representative Councils to canvas young people's opinions. I took those into account when I proposed a number of activities. The proposals I prepared were accepted and funded by the committee. I was directly involved in planning and implementing activities, preparing promotional materials and performing the role of young persons' spokesperson on local radio.

1

OTHER WORK EXPERIE
Delicatessen shift supervisor (
Coleworth supermarket, Sun
Delicatessen assistant (part ti
Coleworth supermarket, Sun

EXTRA-CURRICULAR
Content manager, 2001–2004
Summers Park Tidy Town Co
I was responsible for updati
develop the website's pote
place on the 'What's On' p
Cub Leader, 1997–2000
1st Smithtown Scouts
I was one of three leaders
tuition. I attended several
district at the 1999 natio

INTERESTS
Outside my work and volut
having studies for nine yea
gigs at Smithtown Universi
I enjoy Celtic studies and

REFEREES
Dr Lucy Lane
Senior Lecturer in PR
University of Summer
Phone
Email

Lionel Abbey
Managing Director
Hodges & Hodges
Phone
Email

Chas Scuro
Councilor, Summers Park City Council
(Chairman – Tidy Town Committee)
Phone

2

fyi

Note that you are no longer required to list your age or marital status.

You can see a full-sized version of this résumé in the Appendix.

This resume includes career goals and volunteer work – both important when applying for NFP jobs.

The objective section (stated goals) is a good thing if you are applying for the NFP sector because you show why you want to be there, what your values and motivations are and maybe show some kind of key experience, training or interest, something that is key to the role.

Elizabeth Varley, Director, Challenge Consulting Australia

As for volunteering, this can often be a way of accruing skills and experience in the NFP sector, so don't forget to include these jobs. But you also need to be careful about what kind of experience you include.

> It depends on what the volunteer work involved. It should only play a part in your résumé if it is tailored to the job you are going for.
> Nicole Abate, HR assistant, Mission Australia

Interests and hobbies are another area that you should address.

> The interests and hobbies section can be an anchor for the interviewer to start building rapport, and often it's a way they can work out if you are a cultural fit for that organisation.
> Elizabeth Varley, Director, Challenge Consulting Australia

If the emphasis of the job is on a certain level of skills training or educational qualifications, you can place the education and training section before work experience.

When it comes to layout, your résumé should be typewritten in an easily readable font between 10–14 in size, evenly spaced, with enough white space between sections to allow skimming. And you shouldn't use 'Résumé' as a heading – just use your name!

You should also resist the temptation to use graphics and photos.

Language is also important, so try to use 'key' words that are relevant to the industry in which you are seeking employment.

Lastly, to make your skills stand out, begin sentences or phrases with powerful action verbs. Avoid words like 'assisted', 'helped', 'aided', 'participated' or 'contributed' as they do not say precisely what you did.

Tips: The résumé

- DO spend time working on the layout, sentence structure and content of your résumé as a well-presented résumé can boost your chances of getting the job.

- DO be truthful.

- DON'T plagiarise anyone's work and DON'T exaggerate – it's a waste of time for all concerned.

- DON'T send a résumé that has not been carefully proofread or waste employers' time by applying for positions in the profession that require essential skills and competencies that you do not have.

- Unless an advertisement states that training will be provided, it is taken for granted by a prospective employer that you have the skills.

- Keep your résumé to two or three pages (standard).

- If a company you have worked for may not be well known, include a sentence to explain who they are and what they do.

- Your career history should begin with your most recent job first and then work backwards.

- Check job-search websites for résumé samples and tips.

- Consider using a professional résumé-writing service.

- Write each résumé to fit the job that you are going for.

- Keep the master résumé as an electronic file and update regularly.

- Keep copies of each individualised résumé for referencing when applying for similar jobs.

The cover letter

With application processes increasingly online or facilitated by email, the attention span of a potential recruiter can be as short as that of a goldfish. So, you need to tell them why they should even bother to flip to your résumé, and do so in a short space of time – no more than three paragraphs.

A cover email will address the same requirements as a cover letter but more succinctly, and following different stylistic conventions. This email is particularly brief with one 'sell' paragraph.

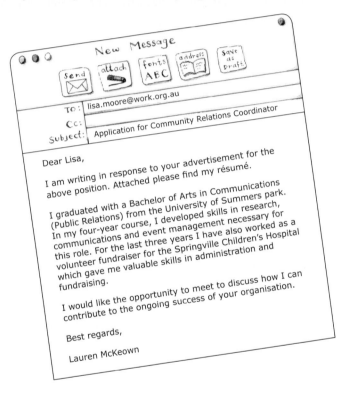

You can see a full-sized version of a cover letter in formal business format in Appendix 5.

When writing your cover email or letter, you should start off with a sentence that mentions the job you are applying for and where you saw it advertised – this is for the benefit of the employer and will be appreciated, especially in a large organisation that advertises for many different positions.

> It has to have something that makes me want to read the entire
> package, something that makes me want to meet the person
> – but without exaggerating!
> Lyn Goldsworthy, NFP consultant

The second sentence can state what you can bring to the role, and
the third should express your interest in not just the position, but the
organisation as a whole.

A second paragraph can expand on this by directly addressing
the criteria for the position. Draw attention to relevant skills,
qualifications and/or experience you have, but make sure you provide
concrete examples.

And the ending? Don't be coy about it. Either say simply that you
look forward to meeting to discuss your potential contribution, or say
what your availability is for an interview and what your next follow-
up contact will be. For example, 'I am available for an interview over
the next two weeks on Mondays between nine and six, on this phone
number. If I haven't heard from you in two weeks' time, I will call you.'
Something like that will definitely keep you at the top of the pile!

Elizabeth Varley warns job seekers to be careful with words that
they are not in the habit of using. One of her young clients, when
attempting to underline how good he was with people, wrote that he
was a very apathetic person when he obviously meant empathetic.

When it comes down to it, this kind of mistake can cost you the job
– you should always proofread for spelling, grammar, punctuation and
typographical errors before you send your application; even better,
get somebody else to give it a second eyeball.

Deborah Tabart from the Australia Koala Foundation agrees that
simple mistakes like this can cost you your chances at getting an
interview. She says that if an applicant gets her name wrong, says
'Dear Sir' instead of 'Dear Madam', or uses bad spelling, she'll just
throw the application away!

Tips: The cover letter

- Tailor the letter to suit the employer.
- Standardise the formatting.
- Don't start every sentence with 'I'.
- Be succinct – one A4 page, well spaced.
- Have a friend proofread your letter.
- Use polite, formal language.
- Be clear, objective and persuasive.
- Back up general statements with specific facts.
- Avoid jargon and clichés.
- Be truthful — do not misrepresent yourself.

Selection criteria

When applying for a job in the NFP sector, you will often need to respond to selection criteria. These are in addition to your résumé and cover letter, and will generally have to be supplied as a separate document.

Selection criteria describe the skills, knowledge and experience needed to do the job.

Your claim for the position is the most important part of your application. The people who best meet the selection criteria will make it to the next stage of the selection process, usually an interview. And the questions you will be asked at an interview will be based on the selection criteria.

In addition to criteria specific to the job, the selection criteria will also include 'common criteria'. These are requirements that apply to all positions and relate to issues such as Equal Employment Opportunity and Occupational Health and Safety. Make sure you give these proper consideration.

Under each criterion you will need to:

- explain how your skills, experience, abilities and personal qualities relate to that criterion and the duties of the role
- give examples of your major achievements which illustrate your claims. Just saying you can do something or that you have had experience is not enough
- include only relevant information
- make your response to each criterion comprehensive but concise.

Tips: Selection criteria

- Be honest – do not make unsupported claims.
- Make sure you understand the key phrases such as 'experience in' and 'knowledge of'.
- Give tangible examples of your claim.
- Make sure the examples are relevant.
- Use direct, active verbs and address all parts of the selection criterion.
- Check to find out the maximum length for each.
- Use bullet (dot) points to show your ability to write concisely and clearly.
- Use language that is relevant to the position but avoid excessive use of jargon.
- Proofread your work carefully and ask someone else to proofread it as well.

How can I stand out at the interview?

Now that your outstanding application has landed you an interview, the serious selling can begin!

Don't panic – interviews need not be an uncomfortable experience. Remember that while you are selling your skills to the interviewer or panel, they should also be selling their workplace to you. Despite popular opinion to the contrary, interviews are a two-way street, and you are in the driver's seat!

There are three rules for standing out at the interview. Actually, it's three Ps:

- preparation
- presentation
- performance.

Preparation
Research the company

- Read or skim the annual report and any other information.
- Find out about the structure of the organisation.
- Get to know the key positions and the names of people in them.

Presentation
Be personable and dynamic

- Focus on your strengths – you'll be less nervous
- Develop a rapport with the interviewer/s
- Dress appropriately and be well groomed
- Speak clearly
- Make eye contact
- Smile, relax, breathe!

Interview 3 Ps

Performance
Find out about interview techniques

- Make sure you answer the question – don't get side tracked!
- Be honest in your responses
- Talking about mistakes isn't a bad thing if you show that you have learnt from them

Preparation

Research, research, research. And, after that, more research. All the employers we spoke to stressed the importance of doing your homework before your interview. This includes finding out as much as you can about the organisation by visiting their website, as well as asking the recruiter for as much information as they can provide on the job.

> It makes a huge difference to tired and grumpy interviewers if candidates seem to know something about the job or company.
> Lyn Goldsworthy, NFP consultant

Trish McDonald, HR officer from CARE Australia, also likes to see that the interviewee has done their research on what makes her organisation different from other aid organisations.

> Research is the big thing for us – that they've got as much information as they can on your organisation and your programs, where your countries are, an idea of your structure and how you work.
> A typical question that I like to ask, to get this kind of information flowing from an applicant, is: 'What is it that differentiates CARE Australia from other international NGOs?' Some people give a really great answer and some people will struggle with that.
> Trish McDonald, Recruitment officer, CARE Australia

As organisations involved in 'saving the world' tend to focus on a particular problem, you also have an additional assignment. Lyn suggests that you look through the last six to 12 months of newspaper articles to familiarise yourself with the issues and formulate your thoughts about the public discussion surrounding them.

You should also practise the interview.

During the first few minutes of the interview, an employer will be formulating their first impression of you. They will do this by noticing the way you greet the employer, the firmness of your handshake and initial eye contact. They may also ask you common-ground questions as a way of establishing a rapport – 'Tell me about yourself' is a common opener.

As silly as it might make you feel, you should practise this part of the interview. Ask a friend, a colleague or a family member to role play the interviewer. Practise your handshake and greeting, your answer to rapport-building questions, and your response to 'tell me about yourself'.

You should also prepare and practise your answers to questions that you will be asked about the job and your application, such as, 'What are some of your key personal strengths?'

> Think about your strengths for the job – and also your weaknesses. Think about what you would need to get on top of the job. Don't be afraid to outline these in the interview.
> Lyn Goldsworthy, NFP consultant

Role play questions

- Why did you apply for this role?

- What will you bring to the role and the organisation?

- Describe your last or current job?

- Why did you choose to pursue a degree in ... ?

- What are your long-term career goals?

Competency and behavioural questions are also common and can often throw people if they are not prepared.

> One of the most reliable ways for an interviewer to project how you would perform in the future is to examine the past. Therefore, many employers prepare behaviour-based questions. Behaviour-based interviewers usually develop their questions around the traits and skills they deem necessary in a position or organisation.
>
> Challenge Consulting Australia

These questions usually begin with phrases like 'Tell me about a time when ... '

Presentation

It's important that you come across as personable and interested in the job. It's okay to be nervous but try to focus on your strengths and what you are saying rather than your nerves.

Job interviews are a balancing act. On one hand you want to demonstrate how your experiences, skills and attributes make you the ideal person for the job. On the other, you don't want to give a false impression about who you are and what you can do. Be clear about who you are and what you can offer.

Present yourself in the best light and show your commitment to your work and that this can translate to improving the delivery of the organisation's services.

Presentation is also about how you look. Think about the job, the organisation and dress appropriately. Dress up a bit more rather than running the risk of looking underdressed. From the moment you arrive, you need to exude a professional manner. Be aware of your body posture and your voice. Speak clearly. Smile. Make eye contact with all you meet and speak with and – don't forget to keep breathing!

Performance

Having practised your meet-and-greet routine, you should have the initial 'warm-up' part of the interview down pat. Another thing to consider when creating those important first impressions is the way you are dressed.

> Be well presented – scruffiness in dress indicates scruffiness in approach to job. This doesn't mean a suit, but it does mean clean clothes that fit, brushed hair, and clean face, fingernails and hair.
> Lyn Goldsworthy, NFP consultant

The interview will then shift into the meat of the exercise – the exchange of information. In this part, how you communicate, verbally and non-verbally, is as important as what you say.

But while you need to be professional in your approach, you should not be afraid to let your personality shine through, and a sense of humour is always welcome. With the emphasis on passionate and compassionate people in the NFP sector, allowing them to see who you are is important.

> I connected with the interview panel on that emotional level where I could display and give examples of my work practice, especially around the psycho-social stuff.
> Dean King, Support services coordinator, Leukaemia Foundation

You may need to leave your soapbox at the door, but your thoughts and opinions on the issues – be it on topics such as environmentalism, social welfare, health, for example – are also welcome. Not only will it make you look prepared but it will also illustrate that you have an understanding and appreciation of the context in which the organisation works.

> Understanding of the issues is also important. If that is apparent in an interview, then it's more likely the interviewee will be rated a bit higher by the panel.
> Trish McDonald, Recruitment officer, CARE Australia

Demonstrating how your skills can be brought to bear on these issues is a sure winner.

> In my interview I talked about ideas for direct action and campaigning and how to work with volunteers. I demonstrated that I had an understanding of how to use non-violent direct action strategies in environmental campaigning.
> Nic Clyde, Actions unit manager, Greenpeace

How you respond to negative experiences in the interview is also important.

> Be prepared to state if you don't know how to answer a question – but offer a way forward – how you might get the information to answer the question. It's much better to be honest than to lie.
> Lyn Goldsworthy, NFP consultant

And if you are asked about a low grade, a sudden job change, or a weakness in your background, don't be defensive, warns Elizabeth Varley.

> Be positive. Employers don't want to hear a litany of excuses or bad feelings about a negative experience. Focus instead on the facts and what you learned from the experience.
> Elizabeth Varley, Director, Challenge Consulting Australia

When you hear the interviewer ask if you have any questions, this is usually a sign that the interview is wrapping up. You should make good use of these closing moments.

> Always ask questions, because this demonstrates your prior research and interest in the job. However, listen carefully during the interview as many of your prepared questions may have been answered.
> Elizabeth Varley, Director, Challenge Consulting Australia

Questions to ask the interviewer

- What do you see as the priorities for someone in this position?

- What do you see as the greatest threats to the organisation?

- Where are the greatest opportunities for the organisation?

- What kind of in-house training opportunities are available?

- How are employees evaluated?

- How would you describe your organisation's management style and working environment?

You should then make sure you understand the next part of the hiring process – ask if there will be another interview and when you can expect to hear about a decision.

> Thank the person interviewing you for their time. Always follow up an interview with a phone call, letter or email of thanks.
> Sam Broughton, Fundraising manager, Salvation Army

Top ten DOs

1 Maintain a positive and confident attitude.
2 Make sure you are well dressed.
3 Listen carefully to questions and instructions.
4 Highlight what benefits you can bring to the company.
5 Use your own real experiences to answer questions.
6 Show passion and enthusiasm for the position.
7 Make sure you promote your strengths and sell yourself.
8 Let the employer know you have a clear career plan.
9 Have an understanding of the job and what will be expected of you.
10 Have a list of prepared questions to ask about the company and the position.

Top ten DON'Ts

1 Don't arrive late to the interview.
2 Make sure you don't mutter or use too many 'umms' and 'ahhs'.
3 Never leave your mobile phone or other electronic devices on.
4 Don't exaggerate your previous experiences or skills.
5 Never arrive unprepared with no knowledge of the company.
6 Avoid talking about negative experiences you have had.
7 Make sure you don't act bored or uninterested.
8 Avoid answering questions with vague or confusing answers.
9 Don't be unprofessional or impolite.
10 Try not to fidget or show how nervous you are.

What can I do right now?

If you've read this far, you're probably ready to begin. There are just a few things you can do to help you get started.

- Network. Get your name out there, and make sure you talk to anyone in the know – in fact, talk to everyone. You never know who might know someone else in the know, you know!

- Do some unpaid volunteer work. If you want to show that you have what it takes to be part of the NFP sector, you have to be able to put your money where your mouth is, so to speak. It will also be a valuable opportunity to make useful contacts, and to get a feel for the NFP culture.

- See the web listings in this book for organisations near you. There's bound to be an NFP organisation in Australia that matches your interests or passion.

- Decide what qualifications you need, then look at relevant programs at universities and TAFE. Check out websites, attend open days, and get in touch – they will normally be more than happy to send you more information about the courses on offer.

- Scour newspapers' job sections and career websites like seek.com for advertised positions.

- Read the news, watch the news, listen to the news – remember that if you want to save the world, you have to keep up to date with what's going on in it.

Good luck!

Buzz words

ACON	The AIDS Council of NSW
AFK	Australian Koala Foundation
AVI	Australian Volunteers International
CRC	United Nations Convention on the Rights of the Child
CSR	corporate social responsibility, or the commitment of businesses to contribute to sustainable economic development, local communities and society at large to improve their quality of life
EPA	Environmental Protection Authority
EWB	Engineers Without Borders
FBT	fringe benefits tax – tax payable by employers for benefits paid to an employee such as a car, mobile telephone or health insurance
get a guernsey	be approved for selection
ICRC	International Committee of the Red Cross
NFP	not-for-profit organisation
NGO	non-government organisation
NRNO	National Roundtable of Non-profit Organisations
OH&S	occupational health and safety
PBI	public benefit institutions
permaculture	creating a sustainable habitat and lifestyle by integrating the principles of ecology, organic gardening, architecture and agroforestry in an ethical way
rapporteur	a person appointed to investigate on an issue and report back to a committee or conference
salary package	to prospectively forego some salary in order to obtain fringe benefits like travel and accommodation
STI	sexually-transmitted infection
UNAIDS	the United Nations agency focused on HIV/AIDS
wellness revolution	the current trend of good living and healthy eating

Appendix 1

University courses

This table is not intended to be an exhaustive list but merely a guide to the sorts of courses that are available in Australia.

New South Wales	
Charles Sturt University	B Social Science (Emergency Management)
	Grad. Cert. in Dispute Management
	Master of Emergency Management
Avondale College	BA in International Development Studies
University of New England	BA, Master of Community Development & Peace Studies
	Adv. Dip. in Civil Care and Security Management
University of NSW	Master of International Social Development
University of Western Sydney	B Community Welfare
Australian Capital Territory	
University of Canberra	Master of Community & Health Development
Australian National University	Master of Environmental Management
	Master of Development Administration
Queensland	
James Cook University	Grad. Dip., Grad. Cert., Master of Tropical Environmental Studies
Southern Cross University	Grad. Cert., Grad. Dip., Master of Community Development (Emergency Management)
University of Queensland	Master of Indigenous Health
	Master of International Studies (Peace & Conflict Resolution)
Victoria	
Deakin University	Master of International & Community Development
Swinburne University of Technology	Grad. Cert. in Disaster Management
La Trobe University	Master of International Policy Studies
Melbourne University	Grad. Dip. in International Health
	Grad. Cert., Master of Development Technologies
	Master of International Development
RMIT University	Master of Social Science (International Urban & Environmental Management)
Victoria University of Technology	Grad. Dip., Grad. Cert., Master of Public Advocacy & Action

South Australia	
Flinders University	Grad. Cert. in Health (Developing Countries)
	Master of Health & International Development.
	Master of Primary Health Care
	PhD in Development Studies
University of South Australia	BA Applied Language & Intercultural Communication
	BSc Biodiversity, Environmental & Park Management
	Grad. Cert. in International Education
	Grad. Dip., Grad. Cert., Master of Water Resources Management
Tabor College	BA, Dip. Intercultural Studies
Northern Territory	
Northern Territory University	Grad. Dip., Master of Community Development & Management
Charles Darwin University	B Welfare Studies
	Grad. Cert. in Sustainable Development
	Master/PhD in Tropical Environmental Management
Western Australia	
Curtin University	BSc (Environmental Health)
	Grad. Cert. in Environmental Toxicology
	Master of International Health
Murdoch University	Grad. Dip., Master of Development Studies
Tasmania	
University of Tasmania	B Regional Resource Management
	B Natural Environment & Wilderness Studies
	Master of Public Administration (International)
	Master of Regional Development Policy
	Grad. Dip. of Natural Environmental Management
	Grad. Dip. of Antarctic & Southern Ocean Studies
	Master of Environmental Planning

Appendix 2

TAFE courses

This table is not intended to be an exhaustive list but merely a guide to the sorts of courses that are available in Australia.

Health & social services	Remote area first aid
	Orientation for overseas health professionals
	Aboriginal & Torres Strait Islander health
	Nursing language (overseas qualified nurses)
	Youth work
	Children's services
	Community welfare
	Disability work
	Drug and alcohol services
	Dispute resolution & mediation/dealing with conflict
	Health (Aboriginal communities)
Environmental management and protection	Conservation & land management
	Water operations
	Forest growing & management
	Ecologically sustainable development
Advocacy, policy & development	Security & risk management
	Government policy development
	Working in the public sector
Emergency, aid & relief work	Crisis management
	Public safety (firefighting & emergency operations)
	Public safety (emergency management)

Appendix 3

Sample job advertisements

Community Relations Coordinator

Do you have established networks?

Do you have the drive, initiative and determination to succeed?

This health foundation is dedicated to defeating disease by building an aware community. We are seeking a dynamic and experienced Community Relations Coordinator to join our regional office and make a real difference to the local community.

Working full-time, this highly satisfying role will see you:

- coordinating local fundraising and high profile events
- engaging the local community through networking and relationship development with donors and supporters
- coordinating local volunteer networks that include dedicated committee groups
- coordinating local media, publicity and promotional activities.

We are looking for a proactive, community motivated and diligent individual who has a demonstrated history of success in:

- growing and coordinating community fundraising events, promotional launches and donor development strategies
- media liaison and publicity generation
- managing and expanding existing supporter and volunteer networks whilst establishing new networks.

If you are someone who has a willingness to learn and accept new challenges, send in your application (addressing the criteria listed above) to jobs@canly.org.au

---

Fundraising Officer
Administrative support for fundraising events and planned giving areas

- Salary – $38,400 equivalent plus super

Our Client is well regarded for providing tremendous support and information to the large number of Australians with diabetes and their families to minimise impact on lifestyle and contribute to the search for a cure. The fundraising business unit generates income to provide education, health promotion and research whilst also raising awareness of the service provided.

The role assists the Fundraising and Planned Giving Manager in the planning, monitoring and development of the entire fundraising plan and has a strong administrative and database focus. You will play a key role in project support of fundraising events, direct mail, trust and foundation submissions, In Memoriam program and independent fundraising.

Key activities of this role will include:

> facilitating the growth of the donor database including appeal mailings, VIP donor system, independent fundraising and donor direct debits

> contributing to the strategy and planning of the fundraising campaigns and suggesting methods of increasing return on investment

> researching and facilitating trust and foundation submissions

> assisting the Fundraising and Planned Giving Manager to plan, monitor and develop the fundraising campaigns; and

> researching areas for funding opportunities.

You will have experience in a similar role requiring you to work on simultaneous projects with multiple supervisors. Experience in the not-for-profit sector and tertiary qualifications in marketing, fundraising or communications would be an advantage. With sound computer skills, particularly Word and database management, you will work autonomously with a hands-on approach and excellent attention to detail.

Apply to info@recruitment.com.

Donor and Campaign Coordinator

Donor Management
Campaign Coordinator

Our client is seeking an enthusiastic, hands on and experienced team member to coordinate the Donor Management System and support the Major Awareness Campaign Manager.

Reporting to the Campaign Manager you need to be a committed and motivated individual with excellent communication and organisational skills.

The successful candidate will need 'Donor Management' or equivalent package experience, provide customer service for donors, recording/receipting of all donations, assist with the management of external partnerships/sponsors and support external fundraising events. You will also be responsible to co-ordinate the schools programs and manage volunteers for the major awareness campaign.

To apply for this role, please email your résumé to info@recruitment.com.au

Make a difference in the life of a child...

Telefundraising

The Hospital Foundation raises funds to invest in initiatives that work wonders for sick children and their families. The foundation offers a fast paced, exciting and rewarding working environment.

We are now recruiting for telefundraisers with experience in outbound phone acquisition programs. We are looking for professionals:

- who can work different shifts
- are flexible and can easily adapt to change
- are outcomes focused, preferably with a sales orientated background
- have a mature outlook
- are team players
- possess good data entry skills
- committed to working in the fundraising / not-for-profit industry
- share the Foundation's values.

Please send your résumé to jobs@hospitalfoundation.com.au

Appendix 4

Sample résumé

Lauren McKeown

44 McDaniel St, Summers Park, VIC 6012
Phone: number here   Mobile: number here
email: lauren.mckeown@isthmus.net

CAREER GOALS

To work for an organisation that is committed to making the world a better place and to add to the success of such an organisation.

EDUCATION

2002–2005: **Bachelor of Arts (Honours)**
(Communications – Public Relations), University of Summers Park

2001: **Higher School Certificate**
Summers Park High School, UAI: 93.4

EMPLOYMENT HISTORY

Volunteer fundraiser, 2003–present

Springville Children's Hospital

In 2004 I identified an opportunity to fundraise in partnership with two local high schools. I secure sponsorship from prominent businesses, wrote the promotional copy for fliers, oversaw the production of posters and coordinated an entertainment event in mid 2005 for secondary students. The event was a great success and raised over $1000 for the Institute.

Intern, November 2004 – February 2005

Hodges & Hodges Public Relations Pty Ltd

I completed a full-time paid internship over the three months of university break with this company. My responsibilities included:
- editing copy for conference brochures
- obtaining quotes from printing companies for various jobs and compiling recommendations for the management team's consideration
- visiting venues to evaluate the suitability for a product launch function
- researching launch campaigns for similar products to ascertain what worked well and what should be avoided
- writing weekly updates for the company's website
- attending agency meetings with clients such as Ring-A-Ding Mobiles, Summers Park Convention Centre and Summers Park City Council.

Youth representative, 1997–2000

Summers Park Tidy Town Committee

In this voluntary role I contributed ideas at monthly meetings to increase youth involvement in planned activities throughout 2000 to celebrate the bicentenary of the town's establishment. Several of my ideas were accepted by the committee.

The highlight was working with local Student Representative Councils to canvas young people's opinions. I took those into account when I proposed a number of activities. The proposals I prepared were accepted and funded by the committee. I was directly involved in planning and implementing activities, preparing promotional materials and performing the role of young persons' spokesperson on local radio.

1

OTHER WORK EXPERIENCE

Delicatessen shift supervisor (part time), 2002–present
 Colesworth supermarket, Summers Park

Delicatessen assistant (part time), 1998–2001
 Colesworth supermarket, Summers Park

EXTRA-CURRICULAR ACTIVITIES

Content manager, 2001–2004
Summers Park Tidy Town Committee website
 I was responsible for updating the website after committee meetings. Taking the initiative to further
 develop the website's potential, I regularly compiled information on forthcoming events in the local area to
 place on the 'What's On' pages of the website. This has proved popular with locals and visiting tourists.

Cub Leader, 1997–2000
1st Smithtown Scouts
 I was one of three leaders for a large troop of cub scouts. I assisted in all activities, camp-outs and skills
 tuition. I attended several leadership training programs through Scouting Australia and represented my
 district at the 1999 national leaders' conference.

INTERESTS

Outside my work and volunteer responsibilities, my interests centre on music. I play piano for relaxation,
having studies for nine years. I'm also a keyboard player in a fringe Celtic revival band that plays occasional
gigs at Smithtown University.
I enjoy Celtic studies and have a strong interest in the Gaelic language.

REFEREES

Dr Lucy Lane
 Senior Lecturer in PR
 University of Summers Park
 Phone
 Email

Lionel Abbey
 Managing Director
 Hodges & Hodges Public Relations Pty Ltd
 Phone
 Email

Chas Scuro
 Councilor, Summers Park City Council
 (Chairman – Tidy Town Committee)
 Phone

2

Appendix 5

Sample cover letter

Lauren McKeown
44 McDaniel St
Summers Park VIC 6012
email: lauren.mckeown@isthmus.net

Lisa Moore
27 Lucretia Ave
Robsonville VIC 3012

Date of letter

Dear Ms Moore

Re: Community Relations Coordinator

Please consider my application for the position of Community Relations Coordinator, advertised in The Age on (add date of advertisement). Enclosed is my résumé for your information.

I graduated with a Bachelor of Arts in Communications (Public Relations) from the University of Summers Park. In my four-year course, I developed skills in research, communications and event management necessary for this role. For the last three years I have also worked as a volunteer fundraiser for the Springville Children's Hospital which gave me valuable skills in administration and fundraising.

I would enjoy talking to you in an interview and look forward to hearing from you.

Yours sincerely

Lauren McKeown

Photo credits

A big thanks goes out to everyone who generously supplied photographs for this book.

Front cover: Christine Nesbitt

'The big picture' chapter divider: Jyn Meyer, stock.xchng

'Insider info' chapter divider: K. Kaveney, Dreamstime.com

'Ready, set, go for it!' chapter divider: Wilhjelm, stock.xchng

Miscellaneous photographs
Amnesty International Australia; Australian Koala Foundation; Silvia Ruggeri; AYAD/ Austraining; Capture Media; CARE Laos; Daniel Almagor; Dean King; Ern Mainka; Ernestine Thompson; Felicity Stafford; Greenpeace; Joshua Estey; Julia Cabassi; Katie Rivers Photography; Mark Reeves; Nami Nelson; Nic Clyde; Nicola Sutherland; RFDS (Central Operations); Sarah Cass-Segaan; Stephen Cannings; Zoe Rudder; Daniel Gardiner; Bob Denelzen (Gurilla/ Dreamstime.com); CARE Australia; Sam Broughton; UNICEF Australia; Jonothan Treagust, World Vision Australia.

Books for every career you can imagine!

Available now at bookstores and on the Career FAQs website

Accounting
Accounting NSW/ACT
Advertising
Allied Health
Building & Construction
Design Professionals
Engineering
Entertainment
Extreme
Fashion
Financial Planning
Going Global
Hospitality
Human Resources
Information Technology
Investment Banking

Landscaping & Horticulture
Law
Law NSW/ACT
Law Victoria
Marketing
Medicine
Nursing
Nursing NSW/ACT
Nursing Victoria
Psychology
Public Relations
Save the World
Teaching NSW/ACT
Travel & Tourism
Weird & Wonderful

Coming soon

@gov.au
Accounting Victoria
Banking
Be Your Own Boss
Beauty & Fitness
Digital Media
Education
Industrial Design
Journalism

Publishing
Scientific Pursuits
Teaching Victoria
The Art World
The Sporting Arena
Working from Home
Working with Animals
Working with Children

Other 'expand your horizons' titles

Going Global

Want to work overseas? The world's your oyster and Career FAQs *Going Global* your guide. You'll find interviews with Australians working in the UK, the US, Canada, the Netherlands, China, Cambodia, Sudan and other nations. We give you all the essentials to get you going, like visas, and tell you what opportunities are waiting to be seized!

Extreme

Imagine standing at the door of a plane ... looking down at the distant earth ... someone telling you to hurry up and jump ... If your reaction is anything other than to curl up on the floor and cry, an extreme career may be for you! From croc farming to underground mine blasting, this book gives you the facts on getting into the most adrenalin-fuelled careers around.

Coming soon!

Be Your Own Boss

If you were the kid making a profit from trading collector cards in the playground, this book is for you! Read interviews with a range of young people who all have one thing in common – they saw an idea, dared to take risks and are now running their own business. Get practical advice from concept to boardroom, encompassing funding, marketing, people management and more.

Weird and Wonderful

Want to stuff animals for a living? How about telling jokes for a job? Career FAQs *Weird and Wonderful* tells you about creative, unusual, humorous and some quite dangerous jobs that will make great conversation at parties. It's essential reading for those who don't just think outside the square, but who want to work there too!

The Sporting Arena

Whether it's your lifelong dream to win gold at the Olympics, or you just watch a LOT of sport on TV, there is a job in the sporting world that's perfect for you. Career FAQs *The Sporting Arena* includes interviews with sportspeople of all sorts about what it's really like to make a career out of pursuing your personal best. We also talk to trainers, managers, sports marketers and journalists and others, so you can learn about the possibilities and how to get started.

SEEK.COM.AU HAPPINESS

The right job can change your life. If you love your job, chances are most other things in your life will fall into place. Finding the 'right' job is a matter of exploring all the options. And no-one can provide you with more job options than **SEEK**, Australia's #1 job site.
SEEK and you shall find!